Osprey Modelling • 30

Modelling the Panther Tank

Steve van Beveren

Consultant editor Robert Oehler • *Series editors* Marcus Cowper and Nikolai Bogdanovic

First published in 2006 by Osprey Publishing

Midland House, West Way, Botley, Oxford OX2 0PH, UK

443 Park Avenue South, New York, NY 10016, USA

E-mail: info@ospreypublishing.com

ISBN 10: 1-84176-928-2

ISBN 13: 978-1-84176-928-8

Page layout by Servis Filmsetting Ltd, Manchester, UK

Typeset in Monotype Gill Sans and ITC Stone Serif

Index by Glyn Sutcliffe

Originated by United Graphics Pte Ltd, Singapore

Printed and bound in China by Bookbuilders

06 07 08 09 10   10 9 8 7 6 5 4 3 2 1

A CIP catalogue record for this book is available from the British Library.

FOR A CATALOGUE OF ALL BOOKS PUBLISHED BY OSPREY MILITARY AND AVIATION PLEASE CONTACT:

NORTH AMERICA

Osprey Direct, C/O Random House Distribution Center, 400 Hahn Road, Westminster, MD 21157, USA

E-mail: info@ospreydirectusa.com

ALL OTHER REGIONS

Osprey Direct UK, P.O. Box 140, Wellingborough, Northants, NN8 2FA, UK

E-mail: info@ospreydirect.co.uk

Acknowledgements

First, I would like to thank my wife Mary and my two children, Anja and Erich, for their support and patience while I worked on this book. Second, I would like to thank my good friends Doug Jameson, Gary Edmundson and Tom Cockle for their help and encouragement throughout the preparation of this book.

I would also like to acknowledge the following people and companies for their help and generosity. Thomas Jentz who supplied me with a diagram of the crew-compartment heater hoses installed in the Panther Ausf. G; Neil Short for the Pantherturm construction drawings he supplied; Don Campbell who provided me with numerous photos of Bovington's Panther Ausf. G interior; Roddy MacDougall for his keen eye when it comes to Panther details; Freddie Leung of Dragon Models Ltd for supplying some of the kits used in this book; Taesung Harmms of Alpine Miniatures for sculpting and converting the figure used on the Panther Ausf. D kit; Yasutsugu Mori of Modeling Artisan Mori who supplied some of the detailed items used in this book; Model Point Barrels for the brass MG34 barrels used on the Panther Ausf. G; Aber for the Panther Ausf. G engine screens; and Armorscale for the excellent Panther Ausf. G Mantlet and barrel.

Photographic credits

Unless otherwise indicated, the author took all the photographs in this work.

Contents

Introduction

The Panther tank has often been referred to as the best tank of World War II. This claim has been made based on the tank's combination of mobility, firepower and armour. Development of this vehicle came as a direct result of requests from the troops for a tank that could deal with the heavy Soviet armour being encountered on the Eastern Front. Initially Daimler-Benz was awarded the contract for the manufacture of the Panther in March 1942. This decision was later overturned and the contract was awarded to MAN in May 1942. This was based partly on the fact that the Daimler-Benz tank required the design of a new turret that would delay its introduction. The MAN chassis, however, utilized a turret design that had already been developed by Rheinmetall, allowing it to enter production quicker. The Rheinmetall turret housed the 7.5cm KwK L/70 that would be with the Panther for its entire production run.

The development of the Panther took just over a year and a half, with the tank having its combat debut in July 1943. This was a remarkably short development phase and meant that the first vehicles suffered from mechanical shortcomings. Final drive failure was a common problem and initially the engine was underpowered. These shortcomings were fixed as the production of the tank went on, right up to the end of the war.

The first production-series Panther was the Ausf. D, of which approximately 850 were produced from January to September 1943. The Ausf. D had a drum-shaped cupola similar to the type on a Tiger I. Italeri was the first company in recent years to release an injection-moulded kit of the Panther Ausf. D (IT290) in the mid-1990s. Unfortunately it was poorly moulded, dimensionally incorrect and suffered from a lack of detail. In 2002 Dragon Models Ltd from Hong Kong released their second kit of the Panther, the Ausf. D (DML6164), which was every-thing the Italeri kit was not. It was well moulded and dimensionally accurate with its only fault being the fixed suspension and idler arms. In 2005 ICM from the Ukraine also released an injection-moulded kit of the Ausf. D (ICM35361). Its overall dimensional accuracy is quite good and it features a separate transmission hatch, engine deck grilles and individual torsion bar arms.

Tom Cockle with the author at Aberdeen Proving Grounds, atop the Panther Ausf. A. (Photo by Gary Edmundson)

The Ausf. A was the next production-series Panther to be produced, from August 1943 to April 1944 about 2,200 were manufactured. The Ausf. A was basically an Ausf. D hull with an improved turret. Pistol ports on the turret sides were removed from production when the *Nahverteidigungswaffe* (close-defence weapon) was introduced in December 1943. Initially the Ausf. A featured the same type of hinged flap for the hull machine gun as the Ausf. D; however, this was changed in November/December 1943 to a ball-mounted machine-gun housing. Tamiya's version of the Panther Ausf. A (TM35065) was originally released in the 1970s as a motorized kit. The addition of the motorization components caused numerous dimensional concessions affecting the accuracy of this kit. In the 1990s Italeri released a version of the Panther Ausf. A (IT270) and it suffered from all the same problems as their Ausf. D kit. In early 2001 DML's first release of a Panther tank kit came in the form of the Ausf. A Early (DML6160), which can be built as a vehicle produced before November 1943. A year or so after that, a later version of the Ausf. A was released by DML to model vehicles built after November 1943.

The last version of the Panther tank was designated Ausf. G and entered production in March 1944. Almost 3,000 were produced before production ceased in April 1945. The Ausf. G featured a simplified hull construction with single-piece side and pannier plates. The turret design was the same as had been designed for the Panther Ausf. A. In the 1980s Gunze Models from Japan released 'High Tech' versions of the Panther Ausf. G; these kits came with numerous brass and white-metal additions along with individual-link tracks. They were fairly expensive and eventually went out of production. In the mid-1990s Tamiya released several different versions of Panther Ausf. G kits. These were extremely well-moulded kits for their day, although research published in recent years has brought to light some inaccuracies of these kits. In the late 1990s DML released several different versions of the Panther Ausf. G based on the old Gunze moulds. These kits had many of the brass and white-metal parts replaced with plastic versions.

Panthers also saw service as recovery vehicles, known as Bergepanthers. Starting in June 1943, 12 Panther Ausf. D chassis were converted to be recovery vehicles. This was simply accomplished by installing some decking where the turret was normally mounted. The second series of Bergepanthers, based on the Ausf. A, entered service in June 1943. This version featured a dedicated hull assembly, a 40-ton winch and 2cm KwK gun mounted on the front hull plate. A jib-boom crane could be mounted on the engine deck and the rear of the vehicle was fitted with a large spade. There were 123 Bergepanther Ausf. As built until October 1944 when production changed over to the Ausf. G, which adopted the same basic hull shape as the Panther Ausf. G. Italeri was the first company to release an injection-moulded kit of the Bergepanther (IT285), which came out shortly after the release of their Ausf. A and Ausf. D kits. It suffered from the same problems as the previously released kits and is now out of production. In 2005 ICM released a kit of the first-series Bergepanther.

Starting in late 1943, Panther turrets were used in static fortifications to guard key positions. These fortifications were called Pantherturms of which there were two types, the Pantherturm I and Pantherturm II. Some production turrets were used but the majority of them were built specifically for their intended use. The turrets produced for these Pantherturms were different from production turrets in that the roof was reinforced and a flat, hinged hatch replaced the cupola. The majority of the Pantherturms were installed on the Western Front and in Italy with some being installed on the Eastern Front. There are three commercially available kits of Pantherturms available, two from MIG Productions (35-013 and 35-014) of Spain and the other from Just Plane Stuff (JPS020).

Using currently available kits and some aftermarket additions I will detail the construction of five separate models. Various techniques of correcting, modifying and scratch building items will be covered in detail, at varying skill levels.

Tools and materials

The different tools and materials described in this section were used during the construction of the models throughout this book.

Airbrushes
A good airbrush is one of the most important tools a modeller can invest in. They allow a finish quality that is difficult to achieve with a brush and are almost essential for painting camouflage schemes. Iwata and Tamiya dual actions are excellent choices and both were used on the models throughout this book.

Styrene sheet, rod and tubing
Sheets of varying thickness and different sizes of rod and tube were used during the scratch building of numerous parts for this book. A large cutting mat and sharp No. 11 X-Acto blades make working with these materials much easier.

Paint pigments and chalk pastels
An effective portrayal of weathered and dirty appearance can be achieved through the use of chalk pastels or paint pigments. Either can be finely ground to allow them to be dusted or painted onto models when mixed with a carrier. Varying levels of dusty or muddy finishes can easily be achieved. Paint pigments were used to create the dirty and dusty finish on the Panther Ausf. A model featured in this book.

Apoxie Clay
This is a two-part epoxy putty that is mixed together at a 1:1 ratio and can be thinned and smoothed out with tap water. Some of its more useful modelling-related applications are creating weld beads, *Zimmerit* and sculpting.

Punch and die sets
These are essential in my opinion for extra detailing and scratch building as they easily allow nut and bolt detail to be created. Though costly to purchase they are well worth the expense.

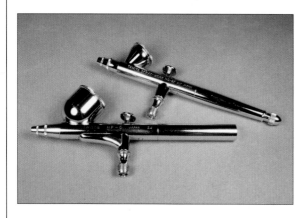

A good airbrush is one of the most important tools a modeller can invest in. Iwata and Tamiya dual actions are excellent choices and both were used on the models throughout this book.

Pre-mixed pigment powders have become a handy weathering tool for modellers. There are several manufacturers of these products including MIG Productions and MMP. Failing the availability of pigments, ordinary chalk pastels can be used as well.

Two-part Apoxie Clay can be used for creating both weld beads and *Zimmerit*, along with filling larger gaps.

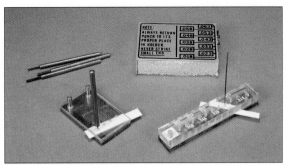

Waldron and Historex punch and die sets were used for adding missing nut and bolt detail.

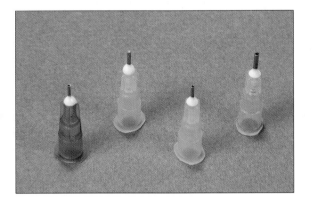

Several different gauges of syringe tips were used for making flush screw head details. By pressing them into the plastic a small circular depression is left; the slot of the screw is then marked with a No. 11 X-Acto blade.

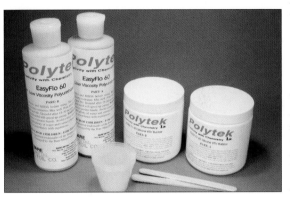

To make multiple copies of parts, Polytek polyurethane casting resin and Platsil 71-20 RTV were used.

Syringe tips
Different gauges of syringe tips, once filed flat and the wall thinned from the inside, can be used to easily create flush screw head details. Simply press the syringe into the plastic creating a circle impression and if required a sharp X-Acto blade can then be used to create the slot. This technique was used to create the missing screw detail on the roof of the DML Panther turrets.

Resin casting and RTV mould making
When numerous duplicates of a part are required for a project, resin casting is the ideal way to make them. Several of the parts used on the models featured in this book were homemade castings.

Soldering
Whenever a strong bond or gap filling is required on metal parts soldering is the best choice. The rear stowage boxes and front fenders of the models in this book were soldered for these reasons.

Etched-metal forming tool
The Hold and Fold and Etch Mate are two of the main types of etched-metal forming tools. These products are essentially clamps that allow the brass to be held firmly while it is being formed. The Hold and Fold was used to form the rear Panther stowage boxes and the scratch-built side fenders on the Panther Ausf. G model.

A cordless butane soldering iron was used for soldering the etched fenders and stowage boxes on the models in this book.

The 8in. Hold and Fold comes in handy when forming long or complex metal parts.

Thin-gauge aluminium and copper sheets

The thin nature of these metal sheets makes them well suited for replicating thin walled items when styrene is unsuitable. The copper material is harder to cut than the aluminium but can be soldered together for a stronger bond. Both these materials were used during the construction of the models in this book.

Corded drill

A Black and Decker $^3/_8$in. chuck corded drill was used for creating some of the parts on the models in this book. It was used in conjunction with a sharp No. 11 X-Acto blade to squarely cut tubing and shape circular objects.

Steel drafting compass

By mounting a pin in the side of the compass instead of a pencil lead, I was able to cut circular objects from sheet styrene with ease. The compass is turned continually until the pin full scores through the styrene. This technique was used to create the openings in the replacement hull roofs for both Panther Ausf. G and Bergepanther models.

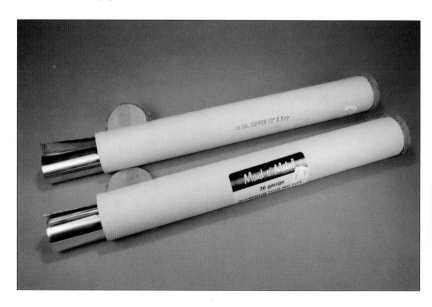

Thin-gauge aluminium and copper sheets, purchased at a crafts store, are used for replicating thin delicate items when styrene is unsuitable.

Panther Ausf. A

Subject:	Panther Ausf. A Early, in Italy with I.Abteilung/Panzer Regiment 4
Kit used:	DML Sd.Kfz.171 Panther A Early Type (Italy 1943/44) kit number 6160
Skill level:	Intermediate
Resin detail sets:	Chesapeake Model Designs CMD-40 Panther Radiator Cooling Fan and Radiators Insert; Modeling Artisan Mori NO-MGP07 Panther Cupola; Plus Model 027 - German WWII Ammo Containers
Etched-metal sets:	Gum Ka GMKT-06 Panther Ausf. A Exterior; Como Models 35B001 Panther A/D Grille set (for Dragon)
Tracks and misc. details:	Friulmodel ATL-08 Panther Late Type Tracks; Karaya TCR01 PzKpfw.V Panther Tow Cable set; Bego 35-002 WWII German Jerrycan set B
Figure:	DML 6191 'Achtung - Jabo!' Panzer Crew (France 1944)
Gun barrel:	Aber 35L04 German 7.5cm Gun Barrel for Panther Ausf. D/A & early G

Introduction

The majority of Panthers sent to Italy in February of 1944 appear to have been produced before December 1943 as they still have hinged machine-gun flaps on the glacis plates and pistol ports on the turret sides. DML's kit of the Panther A Early was used to build one of these vehicles as it comes with all the applicable parts. When building a specific vehicle it's important to carefully study photographs of it, as there were numerous subtle production variations on Panthers. For example some mounting straps for the cylindrical stowage bin were located near the ends and others further in. On page 45 of Daniele Guglielmi's excellent *Panzer in Italy* book there are two photographs of the vehicle I was modelling. After making several notes regarding the features of this vehicle I started with the construction of the kit.

Lower hull and running gear

Assembly of the DML lower hull is straightforward and goes together quite easily. I did, however, deviate from the recommended assembly sequence. Rather than attach the wedge-shaped side plates and sponsons to the upper hull as suggested in the kit instructions, I glued them to the lower hull instead. This deviation allowed a better fit between these parts and the upper hull. I also removed the locating strips from the upper part of the hull sides so that the sponson plates could be aligned with the bottom edge of the sponson extensions on the rear hull plate.

The wheels provided in the Dragon kit are nicely detailed and even have the correct tyre bulge around the rim edge. Once all the wheels had been removed and cleaned up the rubber portion received some distressing with a file. This distressing was done by running a file perpendicularly across the rubber portion of the wheel. As the vehicle I was going to model had been in service for several months before finally being knocked out I thought that the wheels should show some wear.

Panther Ausf. As serving in Italy with I.Abteilung/Panzer Regiment 4 were originally sent to confront the Allied landings at Anzio-Nettuno in February 1944.

The small jerrycan rack next to the left rear stowage bin was made of pieces of a carrier frame from a leftover photo-etch set. As only the upper part of the rack was visible some guesswork was required for the lower part. Jerrycans from the Bego WWII Jerrycan B set were placed in the racks.

Upper hull and turret

The upper hull in the Dragon kit is nicely detailed with crisp moulding all around. It was clearly evident when this kit came out that Dragon intended to release other versions of the Panther tank as the glacis plate was moulded separate from the hull. Test fitting of kit parts before gluing them together is always important as fit problems can sometimes occur if you don't. When test fitting the kit's outer glacis plate to the upper hull, I noticed that the piece

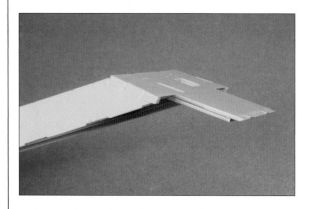

By cutting back the inner glacis plate on the kit, a tight fit between the upper and lower plates can be achieved.

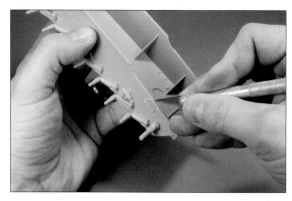

Removing the rear lip on the lower hull allows the sponson to be flush with the rear hull plate.

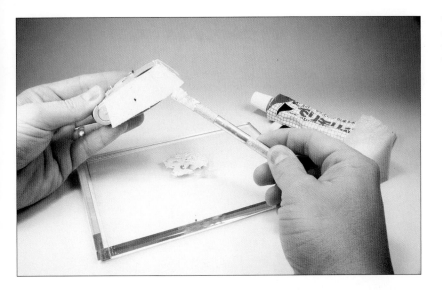

To replicate *Zimmerit* Mori Mori two-part polyester putty is applied to the surface of the model with a wide chisel X-Acto blade.

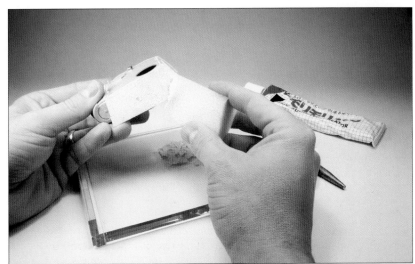

The putty was textured and thinned out using a sponge.

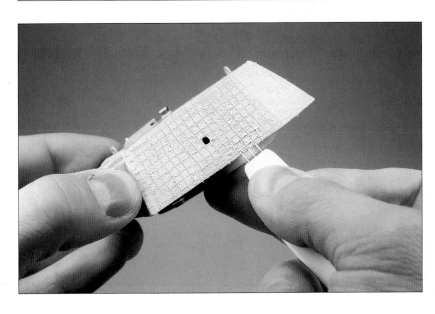

Once the putty is given its rough texture the cross-hatched lines are created with a homemade tool.

Ammo boxes from Plus Models and brass strips were used to replicate the extra stowage boxes seen on Panthers serving with I.Abteilung/Panzer Regiment 4.

The kit's rear stowage boxes were replaced with ones made from thin copper sheet. Also added were the missing tubular conduit cover and rear storage box mounting plate.

behind it looked a little too long. If I mounted the glacis plate pushed tight at the top to the hull sides then I would have a gap at the upper and lower glacis plates. Before gluing the glacis plate onto the upper hull I cut back the inner support for it. This allowed me to get tight seams at all three spots on the front glacis plate.

The cupola provided in the kit is well moulded and it appears to have the correct shape. Unfortunately the openings for the periscopes are too large, as the front edge of the cut-out should be underneath the guard that is welded over it. This is relatively easy to fix with small strips of styrene and Mr Surfacer 500; however, I decided to use the excellent Artisan Mori cupola in place of the kit version. The Mori cupola comes with the correct periscope openings along with periscopes themselves, which are missing from the DML kit. The resin cupola also has the correct internal shape and hatch lever mechanism along with underside detail to the hatch itself. It has been designed to simply replace the kit part and thus fits nicely onto the turret without any extra work.

Most photos of Panthers in Italy show that additional stowage boxes were mounted over the rearmost rectangular grilles. The mounts for these are

Artisan Mori's excellent Panther cupola was painted on the inside before it was attached to the kit.

CMD's Panther radiator fan insert, once painted and weathered, fills the area under the kit's grilles nicely.

visible in the photos of the vehicle I was modelling, though the boxes are not. I again used the leftover brass frame from a photo-etch set to construct the mounts, over which I placed boxes from a Plus Models German WWII Ammo Containers (027) set.

Zimmerit

With the turret and hull now complete it was time to turn my attention to replicating the *Zimmerit*. There are several options for modellers when it comes to replicating *Zimmerit*. It can be created with putty applied over the surface of the kit or by carving it into the plastic with a pyrograph. A few years ago modellers were introduced to another method in the form of pre-sized thinly cast resin sheets. Currently there are two companies that make these resin sheets, ATAK and Cavalier. These sheets have never interested me because the patterns are generally too neat and orderly and they require too much gap filling at the joints between them.

The vehicle I decided to model had the type of *Zimmerit* pattern typical of Panthers produced by Daimler-Benz and MNH. This pattern consisted of a

Nothing adds a sense of scale to a model kit better than a figure. Here a DML figure from the 'Achtung Jabo' set was used, with the head replaced by one from Alpine Miniatures.

Friulmodellismo Metal Tracks (ATL-08) and an Aber Aluminium Barrel (35L04) replaced the less accurate kit items.

Gum Ka photo-etch detail sets were used for the kit's engine screens and tool racks.

roughly applied paste with a series of horizontal and vertical lines scored into it. I decided the best way to replicate it would be to spread out the putty, push in the texture with something rough and then rake the surface to create the horizontal and vertical grooves. Initially I tried a regular scouring pad but unfortunately this created too rough a texture and the small fibres of the pad got stuck in the putty. I then tried small pieces of roughly torn sponge to texture the putty and was very happy with the result. To create the scored lines in the surface of the putty a small tool was made by gluing three sewing pins between two sheets of 1mm styrene sheet. This distance required between the pins was calculated from a period photo of a Daimler-Benz Panther *Schürzen* plate and by counting the number of grooves. This number was then divided into the 1/35-scale dimension for a plate to come up with a spacing of 2.5mm. The pins were then raked across the surface both horizontally then vertically scoring lines into the putty.

When replicating *Zimmerit* using the putty method, it is important to work on one area of the model at a time so as to not destroy one's previous work. I first started on the lower hull, completing both sides in one sitting. After this area had dried I started on the upper hull, completing the glacis plate first then working my way around the model. Once this was done I turned my attention to the turret. The most difficult part here was getting a nice appearance to the *Zimmerit* on the rear part of turret. There are quite a few fittings to work around, but with some care I was able to achieve a result I was happy with. I found it best to leave the harder areas till last, as I was more experienced working with the paste.

Painting

It's debatable as to whether Panthers serving in Italy during autumn 1943 and spring 1944 had any camouflage applied over the *dunkelgelb* basecoat. Period photographs of these vehicles sometimes show what appears to be a camouflage pattern but it is hard to discern if there is one for certain. This could be due to a heavy layer of mud and dust covering the surface of the vehicle. As I had chosen a specific vehicle to model, 415 of I.Abteilung/Panzer Regiment 4, I studied the photos of this vehicle very carefully. Unable to see any camouflage pattern in the two photos of this vehicle I chose not to add one.

When I start the painting process the first thing I do is prime the model with light grey enamel paint. This layer of paint is especially important when different media are used in the construction of the model, such as brass and white styrene. It is also an excellent way of seeing any flaws such as glue marks or scratches in the plastic that may have been previously overlooked. After this initial application of paint has dried I switch to using acrylics. A dark brown paint was made from a mixture of Tamiya Black (XF-1) and Flat Earth (XF-52) that was then sprayed into all the recessed areas and panel edges on the model. The mixture was also applied heavily to areas of the model such as the running gear and around the lower hull. By 'pre-shading' the model in this way fewer washes will need to be used later on. The rubber portion of the roadwheels was sprayed with Tamiya German Grey (XF-63), as using straight black is too stark at 1/35 scale.

Next, Tamiya XF-60 Dark Yellow, lightened with XF-2 White to a ratio of 75 to 25 per cent, was sprayed over the entire model. It's important to apply this layer of paint in a way that allows the 'pre-shade' layer of paint to still show through in a subtle way. A drafting circle template was used to mask the rubber portion of the roadwheels while painting the wheels. Simply find a circle that has a matching diameter for the portion of the wheel that needs to be painted.

Unable to find decal markings for the vehicle I was modelling and due to the fact that they were going to be applied over a rough surface I decided to make my own stencils. I measured the side plate of the DML turret and drew this shape in AutoCAD, which is a computer-aided drafting program. Then I drew

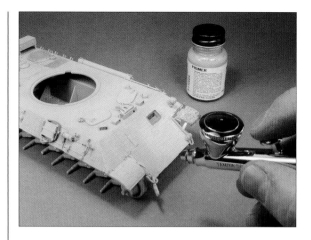

Floquil Grey Primer is sprayed over the entire model to create a uniform tone.

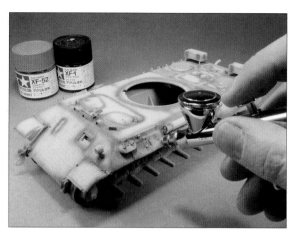

Pre-shading of the model was done by applying a mixture of dark brown made from Tamiya Flat Earth (XF-52) and Flat Black (XF-1).

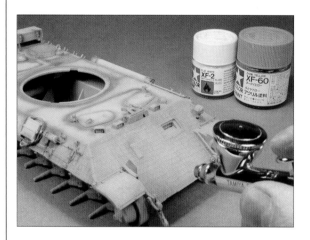

Tamiya Dark Yellow (XF-60), lightened with a little Flat White (XF-2), was applied as the main basecoat of *dunkelgelb*.

With the main basecoat complete the model was given a satin finish.

The extra stowage boxes were carefully masked off and sprayed with Vallejo Panzer Olive Green (096).

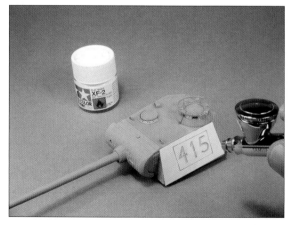

The main portion of the vehicle number was airbrushed through a homemade stencil.

the numbers and was able to play with the scale until they closely matched the size and shape of ones seen on the vehicles in Italy. When I was happy with the size of the numbers I printed out a sheet for both the left and right sides of the turret. The numbers were then cut out from each sheet creating a stencil. Low-tack spray adhesive was applied to one side and they were placed onto the turret. Tamiya Flat White (XF-2) was sprayed at low pressure (10–15psi) through the stencil onto the surface of the model. I then filled in the majority of the white with Vallejo Red (029), painted by hand, leaving only a small border of white around the red. A similar method was used for creating the *Balkenkreuz* on the sides and rear of the lower hull; however this time I used a set of photo-etch stencils made by Fine Molds of Japan. The photo-etch set provides you with a stencil for both the white and black area separately. I found it easier to just use the stencil for the white portion and paint in the black by hand, again using Vallejo paints. The last thing I did during this stage of painting was to provide a light satin sheen to the model. This was achieved by spraying the model with Polly Scale Satin Finish. This satin finish accomplishes two things for me: firstly it provides a nice smooth surface for the washes to follow and second, when not covered completely, it contrasts nicely with the 'matt' finish of weathering to follow.

The Friulmodel tracks were painted with Tamiya German Grey (XF-63). I then lightly sprayed separate applications of thinned Tamiya Flat Earth (XF-52) and Buff (XF-57) in random patterns. This creates a nice starting point for the additional weathering to come.

Weathering

This is the most enjoyable part of the painting process for me as it's where the personality of the model is created. Generally I approach this stage of the model in the same manner; however, I will change the order around or redo certain stages until I am happy with the final result.

I started by making a dark brown wash of Winsor & Newton Raw Umber mixed with mineral spirits. This was applied to all the recessed areas of the kit and around protruding objects. The lower hull and wheels were also washed with this same mixture but it was applied more heavily than on the upper portions of the model. Care must be taken during this stage so as not to darken the overall appearance of the paint finish. The same earth tone colours that were applied to the tracks were now applied to the model itself. Tamiya Flat Earth (XF-52) mixed with isopropyl alcohol, at a ratio of 25 per cent paint to 75 per cent alcohol, was sprayed around the lower hull and onto the wheels. Over this a similarly thinned mixture of Tamiya Buff (XF-57) was randomly targeted to areas of the vehicle that would accumulate dust, such as around the commander's cupola, front fenders and on the engine deck. A very light coating of Tamiya Buff (XF-57) was also sprayed over the entire upper hull. Not only does this provide an overall dusty appearance but the markings are also subtly blended with the rest of the model.

To simulate worn and chipped paint, I first mixed together a slightly lighter version of the base colour using Vallejo Model Color paints. This colour was then randomly applied to areas of the model that would see wear or were supposed to be damaged. Over this I then applied a dark brown colour from Vallejo, leaving edges of the lighter yellow colour to show through. This gives more depth to the chipped paint effect. To further enhance a worn paint look, graphite shavings from a drafting pencil sharpener were rubbed around hatch openings.

The middle row of roadwheel rims always appear shiny in period photographs, due to contact with the track guide horns. To simulate this, the rims of the roadwheels were first drybrushed with Humbrol Super Enamel Camouflage Red (160) then with Testors' Aluminium (1181). Again it's important to leave some of the red colour showing through closer to the centre of the wheel so that the wear appears to have depth.

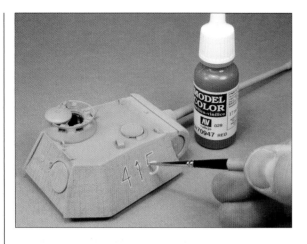

With the white portion of the number dry the centre of the number is filled in with Vallejo Red (029).

Applying decals over this type of *Zimmerit* would be rather difficult so the *Balkenkreuz* was applied through a Fine Molds etched stencil.

To start the weathering process, Tamiya Flat Earth (XF-52) was sprayed around the lower hull.

Tamiya Buff (XF-57) was sprayed in a random pattern around the upper hull to portray collected dust.

A wash of raw umber oil paint thinned with mineral spirits was applied around raised details and panel lines.

Vallejo paints were used to create a chipped paint effect.

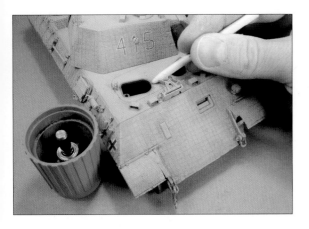

Pencil lead shavings were applied around hatch openings to represent a worn metal look.

To portray the wear pattern seen on Panther roadwheels, the rim was first painted a primer colour with Humbrol Super Enamel Camouflage Red (160). Over this Testors' Aluminium (1181) was drybrushed.

MIG Productions' pigments were applied to areas that would accumulate dust.

To apply the pigments to the wheels they were first painted with isopropyl alcohol. MIG Productions' pigments are then dabbed into the still-wet isopropyl alcohol.

A mixture of isopropyl alcohol and Model Master Acrylic Flat are painted onto the tracks, and then MIG pigments are pushed into the still wet mixture.

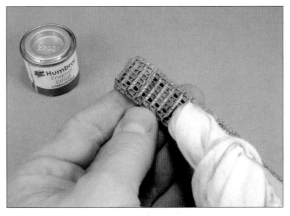

Humbrol Metal-Cote Matt Aluminium (27001) is rubbed over the tread surface of the tracks using a cloth.

To create the look of a fuel spill, Tamiya Clear Orange (X-26) and Smoke (X-19) are mixed together and painted around the filler port.

Gunze Oil (H342) was painted around the hubs of the roadwheels to portray leaking seals.

Next I mixed together a medium brown colour using 'Beach Sand' and 'Europe Dust' from the MIG Productions pigment range. Mixing them together I toned down each of the colours as I find them a bit too stark on their own but I still do get small spots of a single colour appearing every once in a while. These small spots of individual colour provide a nice random pattern to the dirt and mud. To apply the pigments around the lower hull, wheels and tracks I first mix together, at a 1:1 ratio, isopropyl alcohol and Model Master Flat Clear from their acrylic paint line. This mixture was then painted onto the model where I wanted to later apply pigments. To apply the pigments I picked up a small amount with another paintbrush and then pushed it into the still-wet acrylic mixture. This process can be repeated over a previous application to vary the thickness of the pigments. By not mixing the acrylic clear and pigments together and then applying to the model I find that a much grainier texture is achieved. I also find this method allows more control in applying the pigments because if I am not happy with the position of the acrylic clear I can simply let it dry, then paint it on again.

ABOVE Almost 2,200 Panther Ausf. As were produced from August 1943 until April 1944.

BELOW A spattered mud effect was created on the rear of the hull by running my finger across an old toothbrush that had a mixture of pigments and isopropyl alcohol on it.

The Panther tank had a combat crew of five.

The spare track links were painted a primer colour then lightly covered in Rustall and the same pigments that were applied to the roadwheels.

Each of the towing shackles received an application of paint chips and pencil lead shavings.

ABOVE Rustall was applied to the tow cables after they were painted.

BELOW The Panther Ausf. A had a combat weight of 44.8 tonnes.

Panther Ausf. D

Subject:	Panther Ausf. D. at Kursk serrving with the 4th Company of the 51st Panzer Abteilung
Kit used:	DML Sd.Kfz.171 Panther D (Kursk Offensive, July 1943) kit number 6164
Skill level:	Advanced
Resin detail sets:	Tiger Model Designs 352091 Panther D Cupola w/Interior; MIG Productions MP 35-042 Early Panther D Grilles
Etched-metal sets:	Part P35071 Sd.Kfz.171 Panther Ausf. D; Part P35066 Sd.Kfz.171 Panther Ausf. D/A – Fenders; Part P35067 Panther Ausf. D/A Side Skirts
Tracks and misc. details:	Modelkasten SK-13 Panther Early Model Track set; Modelkasten KW-3 Panther Ausf. D Road Wheel set; Karaya TCR01 PzKpfw.V Panther Tow Cable set; Moskit 35-02 Panther Ausf. D Metal Exhaust Pipes
Figure:	Alpine Miniatures 35030 Waffen-SS Panzer Officer (converted to Heere commander)
Gun barrel:	Fine Molds MG-45D Panther 7.5cm Gun Barrel

Introduction

In July 1943 during Operation *Zitadelle* the Panther tank's combat debut occurred, with the 51st and 52nd Panzer Abteilung. A total of eight companies consisting of 192 tanks were fielded. The 4th Company's tanks were marked with large black numbers, outlined in white, on the sides and back of the turret. Unlike the other companies, the 4th had neither a panther's head nor body marked on the turret.

Dragon Models' second version of the Panther to be released was the Ausf. D. It's quite a good kit and can be built out of the box to accurately represent one of the versions of the Panther used during the Kursk Offensive. In the months preceding the offensive, numerous production changes occurred where features were dropped and others added. One area of change was on the type of circular grilles mounted on the engine deck. Initially each of the two radiators had their own filler port, which was cast off one side of the circular grille. These filler ports were later combined into a single one at the rear of the engine deck plate so these cast ports were partially removed with a cutting torch from the grilles. Later on new grilles were cast without this port, which is the type of grille provided by DML.

Lower hull and running gear

Work on the lower hull started by removing both of the moulded-in-place idler arms with a razor saw. To protect the surrounding detail I first masked off the area around the arm with Tamiya masking tape. Once the arms were removed I filed the kit parts so they had a correct shape to the backside and added some short sections of styrene tube so the parts could be mounted back onto the lower hull. To enable the idlers to be re-attached to the lower hull I drilled 4.7mm holes in the hull sides; so the holes were in the same position on both sides a small jig was made. With the holes drilled, new collars for each side were made from 5.5mm (O.D.) styrene tube. The short sections of tube were cut square by

sizing them while mounted in a drill rotating at slow speed. Bolt heads were made, using a Historex hexagonal punch and die set, and then glued around the collar to finish off this area.

The Panther Ausf. D was the first version to see combat, during Operation *Zitadelle* in July 1943.

Modelkasten currently produces a set of early Panther roadwheels for converting Tamiya's Panther Ausf. A kit to an Ausf. D. As I had already purchased these wheels before the DML kit was released, I was able to compare them to the kit's offering. In my opinion the Modelkasten wheels are slightly more defined than the DML versions so I decided to use them instead. Using the Modelkasten wheels, which are designed for the Modelkasten tracks, also meant I didn't have to modify the centre run of DML roadwheels because they are too wide for the tracks. I did, however, have to adapt the Modelkasten wheels to the DML torsion bar arms. This was done by adding small strips of 0.25mm x 0.5mm styrene glued at four places inside the hub. The kit idler wheels are too wide for the Modelkasten tracks so kit part number D2 was sanded down on the backside about 0.5mm before attaching to its mating part, D3. I also added the missing grease nipple ends and I thinned out each of the webs on the idler wheels, as they look too thick when compared to the actual item.

There were two approved designs for interlocking the wedged-shape and upper side plates together, on Panther Ausf. D and A hulls. The DML kit appears to have the *Wahlweise Ausführung* (optional model), which results in a much wider weld joint. The vehicle I was modelling had the standard version of joint, which has a much smaller visible weld bead throughout the interlock area. To replicate this joint, small sections of 0.5mm square styrene were glued into the joints and blended into the existing kit surfaces, using Squadron white putty.

Upper hull and turret

Visible, lying on the ground, in one of the photographs of the vehicle I was modelling was an air cleaner for the HL 210 P30 engine. As this engine was only installed in the first 250 Panther Ausf. D produced it meant that certain features should be present on my model such as the air intake armour caps, which had prongs instead of wire handles. These were scratch built from sheet styrene. To round the edge evenly I glued each of the discs to a styrene tube of the same diameter. This was then mounted in my drill and the edge rounded off while the part was spinning at low speed. It was also a safe bet that this vehicle also had the earlier asymmetrical grilles; therefore MIG Productions' asymmetrical circular grilles replaced the kit parts. I also removed the rain

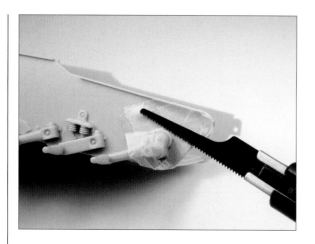

One fault of the DML kit is the fixed idler arms. Therefore the kit's idler arms were removed so workable versions could be added.

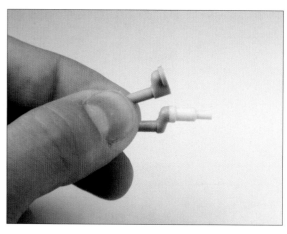

With the idler arm removed styrene tube is then added to the back part. This will allow it to be re-attached to the model.

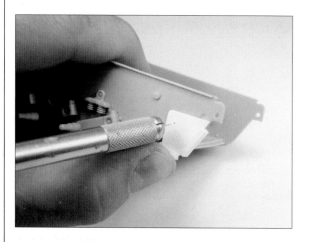

To ensure that both holes for the new idler arms are in the correct position a small jig to locate the holes was made.

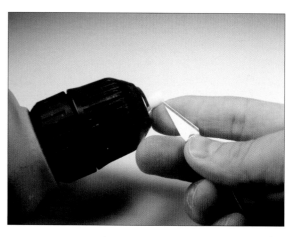

An outer collar for the workable idlers was made by cutting off a piece of styrene tube while being turned in a drill.

The five mounting bolts around the idler collar were made using the Historex hexagonal punch and die set.

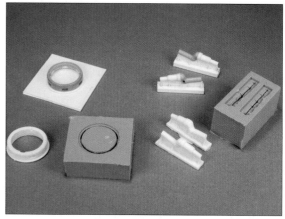

Masters for the idlers and cupola ring were constructed using the kit parts. RTV moulds were then made and copies cast.

After the clay has been applied over the kit weld bead it was smoothed out with water.

A small ball-tipped burnishing tool is used to impart half-moon impressions in the soft clay.

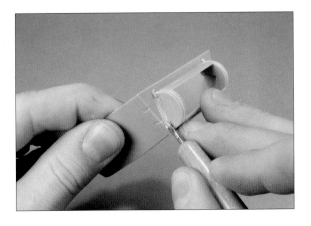

Apoxie Clay is used to blend the trunion housing into the turret front plate.

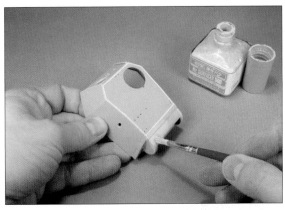

The front of the Panther turret was one large casting. So I lightly stippled Mr Surfacer 500 over both the kit parts to impart a cast texture.

The kit's sideplate and sponson interlock joint is the *Wahlweise Ausführung* (optional model), which results in a wider weld joint. This area was modified to match the specific vehicle I was modelling.

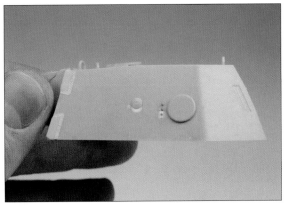

The pistol port on the left-hand side of the turret is too low so it was relocated to the correct position.

The interior parts from Tiger Model Designs' Panther D cupola set were mounted inside a homemade cupola ring casting.

To adapt the Modelkasten wheels to the DML kit, small strips of styrene were glued inside the hub.

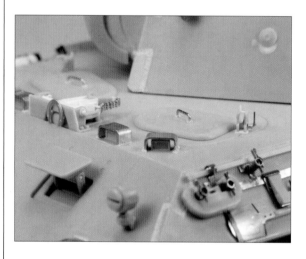

A piece of small, flat brass was used to make the periscope covers as the kit parts are too thick.

Before removing the photo-etch parts from the carrier they were annealed.

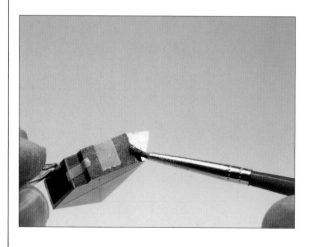

Flux is applied to the joint with a paintbrush.

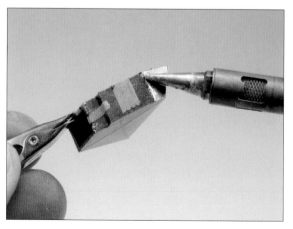

Using a cordless butane soldering iron the solder is carefully applied.

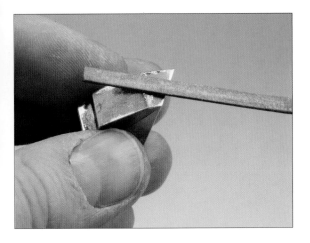

Once the metal has cooled it can be filed smooth.

The stiffening ribs on the face of the stowage bin were embossed with a ballpoint pen before soldering.

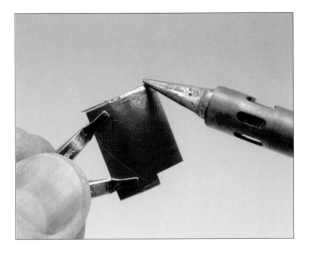

After the front fenders have been shaped and the joint covered with flux, solder is applied.

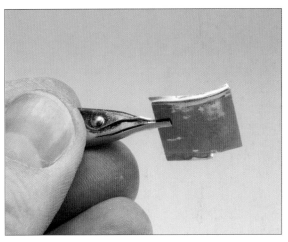

The finished fender ready for embossing of the stiffening ribs.

Due to the small nature of Part's photo-etch *Schürzen* brackets they were 'tinned' before removing them from the carrier.

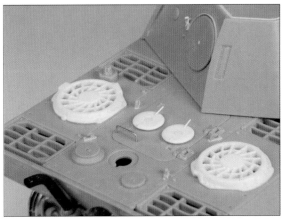

MIG Productions' early asymmetrical cooling fan covers were used instead of the later versions included in the kit.

Small square pieces of 0.25mm-thick styrene were glued onto the back of the etched stowage bins. This allowed them to be attached to the kit with plastic cement.

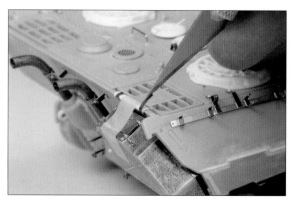

With the stowage bins attached, the vertical hanger strips were formed over a jig.

guard around the fuel filler cap as this was not added until August 1943 and is therefore inaccurate for a Kursk-era Panther.

In reality the front plate and trunnion housing of the Panther turret was one large casting; however, the DML kit supplies these as two separate parts, which results in an incorrect appearance. To correct this I blended the trunnion housing into the front plate using Apoxie Clay, a 'two-part' epoxy putty. A 1.5mm-diameter burnishing tool was used to push the putty into the corner between the front plate and sides of the trunnion housing. A small amount of putty was also used to build out the top right corner of the turret front plate. Once the putty had hardened the whole front plate area was coated with Mr Surfacer 500. This lacquer-based, liquid putty has a granular texture to it and is perfect for creating a scale cast texture. As the putty/paint is drying it can be stippled with a paintbrush to varying degrees of texture.

The pistol port on the left side of the DML turret is about 1mm too low, so the hole was plugged using a tapered piece of 3.2mm styrene rod. This was then cut flush to the side plate of the turret and Squadron white putty applied to blend the parts together. Once this was dry, the correct location for the pistol port was marked and a hole drilled to allow the kit pistol plug to be installed. All of the pistol ports were left loose so that their orientation could be changed once the markings were applied.

The cupola ring that DML provides is moulded in two halves with the join going through the middle of the vision block openings, which results in a nasty seam unless it's filled properly. Apoxie Clay was used for filling this seam as it won't harm the plastic like Squadron putty and it stays workable for a much longer period. Knowing that I would be building more Panther Ausf. D tanks in the future, I decided to make a mould of this assembled cupola ring, but more on that later.

With the hull and turret now complete, I turned my attention to correcting and adding weld beads. Many of the welds on the DML kits are recessed too deep, which is quite noticeable when compared to the real thing. Missing from the DML kit are the prominent welds between the front glacis plates and hull sides, along with the rear hull plate and hull sides. I also needed to add weld beads to the reworked joint at the wedge-shaped hull side and sponson area. To create the weld beads I used Apoxie Clay. I find that it works especially well for creating weld beads because adding water to it can extend the working time. In corners, it's applied to the model using a burnishing tool that allows a consistent fillet of putty to be applied. Where the kit welds are too deep, the putty was pushed into the trough and smoothed out with water. Once the putty was in place I then used a slightly smaller burnishing tool that was pressed into the putty at small intervals. This creates small half-moon ridges in the putty just like what you see in real weld beads. During this process it's important to keep the tool wet so as not to have it stick to the putty and lift it off the model.

Resin casting

Rather than redo the work I had done on the idlers and cupola ring for this model on any of the next DML Panther kits I build, I decided to make RTV rubber moulds of the already completed parts. My RTV of choice is Polytek Platsil 71-20 as it's pliable enough when cured to allow easy part removal, yet is strong enough not to tear. The casting resin I use is EasyFlo 60, also from Polytek, a super low viscosity polyurethane resin that has about a five-minute working time. The extremely low viscosity creates bubble-free castings and pours easily into the moulds. These products are both available in small quantities from Bare Metal Foil (http://www.bare-metal.com).

The first thing that is required when making moulds is to decide the best way for the parts to be orientated so as to avoid two-part moulds if possible. It's also important to take into account how the part will be removed from the mould and any resin carrier. For example, the cupola ring was mounted on a slightly smaller ring of styrene so that when the casting was sanded away from the carrier part detail was not lost. The idlers were each mounted on thin sheets of styrene with reinforcing webs on each side. These webs not only supported the idlers during the mould-making process but also became grooves in the mould that aided in the flow of resin during casting. The next step is to build four walls around the part to contain the RTV rubber during the mould creation. It's important to leave enough room around the parts so that the RTV rubber can be worked into all the crevices of the parts. The area left around the part also needs to be large so that the mould will be thick enough to allow handling during the casting and part-removal process. To work the RTV rubber into all the nooks and crannies of the masters I used a toothpick. Filling in the mould box should be done slowly so that air can escape from the RTV rubber. If the box is filled too fast, air bubbles will form around the part and poor castings will result.

When the RTV rubber moulds had cured for at least 24 hours the masters were removed and copies could then be cast. A tip I picked up from Steve Zaloga is to lightly coat the mould in talcum powder before pouring in the resin. The talcum powder wicks the liquid resin into all the smaller areas of the mould and it also aids in the removal of the casting. During the casting of the parts, any visible air bubbles were removed from the still-liquid resin with a toothpick. After about 20 minutes the resin was hard enough to be removed from the mould.

Moskit hollow metal exhausts (3502) replaced the plastic kit parts.

Up until June 1943 smoke dischargers were mounted on the left and right sides of the turret.

Modelkasten SK-13 Panther early model workable tracks were used on the model.

Due to the smaller diameter of the resin grilles the Part photo-etch grille was re-sized and a brass wire was soldered to the perimeter.

Soldering

Panther fenders are often seen bent and damaged in period photographs and this is easier to replicate with etched fenders than the plastic kit parts. Part's photo-etched fender set (P35066) comes complete with the hull-mounted fenders as well as the fender extensions. As both the fenders and extension require embossing of the raised stiffening ribs, the parts were first annealed before they were removed from the carrier sheet. To anneal the etched fenders, the carrier sheet was set on a hot stove element. This reduces the risk of overheating the smaller etchings and obliterating them from the carrier. It's easy to tell when the sheet has been heated enough, as the colour will change. At the same time I also annealed each of the rear stowage bins included in the comprehensive Part etched Panther (P35071) detail set. Each of the bins comes as a single piece that is folded to form the main body of the bin. The fenders have to be soldered together as it's the only way to get a smooth yet strong joint between the main surface of the fender and the sides. I also decided to solder the rear stowage bins together for the same reasons.

The long tube mounted on the left side of the hull was used to carry spare radio antennas and the gun-cleaning rods.

The track-guard extension and driver's guides were both stored over the fixed portion of the track guard when not used.

All of the parts that needed to be soldered were done in one sitting. Each of the parts was mounted in a small copper clip for ease of handling. The joints on the fenders and stowage bins were carefully coated in flux, taking care not to apply it where it wasn't required. Flux aids in the flow of solder as wherever it is, solder will end up. Using my cordless butane soldering iron, a small amount of solder was applied to each of the joints. If not enough is applied at first then the joint can be recoated in flux and more solder applied. I find this method easier than trying to remove excess amounts of solder later on. Once the parts had cooled, they were filed smooth and the embossing of the strengthening ribs on the fenders was done using a ballpoint pen.

Due to the small nature of Part's photo-etch *Schürzen* brackets they were 'tinned' before removing them from the carrier. This allowed me to hold the small hooks and hanger arms together with flux and simply apply heat to the joint with the soldering iron.

Painting and weathering

I decided on a single camouflage scheme of *dunkelgrün* RAL 6003 over *dunkelgelb* RAL 7028. This type of finish was chosen because I was unable to discern any difference in tones of the camouflage colour in the period photographs. The model was first basecoated with Floquil's Grey Primer to provide a neutral and uniform finish. Pre-shading was then done using a dark brown mixture of Tamiya Black (XF-1) and Flat Earth (XF-52). Over this Tamiya Dark Yellow (XF-60) lightened with Tamiya Flat White (XF-2) at a ratio of 75 to 25 per cent was lightly sprayed over the model. The single camouflage colour was applied using Vallejo Model Air Tank Green (011).

All the vehicle markings were applied using dry transfers from Archer Fine Transfers. After positioning each marking, a small piece of Tamiya masking tape was used to hold it in place while it was rubbed down with a pencil. With all of the markings in place the entire model was covered with Polly Scale Satin Finish, which sealed both the markings and underlying paint. Tamiya Flat Earth (XF-52) and Buff (XF-57) were randomly sprayed around the lower hull, *Schürzen* and onto the wheels. Next the model was given a light wash of Winsor & Newton Raw Umber thinned with mineral spirits. Vallejo Model Color paints and a fine-tipped brush were used to create a light application of paint chips over the surface of the model.

Pigments were then lightly applied around the lower hull and on the horizontal surfaces of the model. Mud splatter on the front and rear of the vehicle was made by collecting a small amount of pigments mixed with isopropyl alcohol on a toothbrush. I then ran my finger across the toothbrush, which causes the bristles to fling the mixture onto the model in small droplets.

A custom-made stencil was used to protect the rubber part of the tyre while applying the main colour.

The single camouflage colour was applied using Vallejo Model Air Tank Green (011). The Model Air line of paints is pre-thinned for airbrushing.

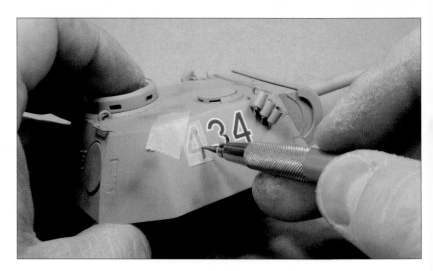

All markings applied to the model were from Archer Fine Transfers' dry transfer line of products.

ABOVE The exhaust pipes were lightly weathered to impart a 'new' look to the vehicle.

BELOW With the rear idler now workable a realistic track sag was easily achieved.

The spare track links were first painted Tamiya German Grey (XF-63) then lightly covered with Dark Yellow (XF-60), being careful to vary the coverage on each link.

Schürzen were mounted to protect the lower sides of the vehicle from Russian anti-tank rifles.

The commander is a converted Alpine Miniatures figure. He was changed from an SS to Heer Panzer officer by Taesung Harmms and painted by the author.

ABOVE The steel portion of all the tools were painted with Humbrol Metal-Cote Gunmetal (27004), which goes on black, then is buffed to a metallic sheen.

BELOW The model was marked as vehicle number 434 of the 4th Company of Panzer-Abteilung 51.

Panther Ausf. G late version (March/April 1945 MAN production vehicle)

Subject:	Panther Ausf. G March/April 1945 production version
Kit used:	Tamiya Panther Type G Late Version kit number 35176
Skill level:	Master
Resin detail sets:	CMK interior sets 3028, 3029 and 3030
Etched-metal sets:	Aber 35024 Panther Ausf. G; Aber 35A79 German Tank Radio set Fu2 & Fu5; Aber 35A93 German Clasps & Clamps (2 choice); Aber 35A91 Rear Boxes for Panther & Jagdpanther; Aber 35G14 Grilles for Sd.Kfz.171 Panther, Ausf. G Late Model
Tracks and misc. details:	WWII Productions 35001 Panther Six Chevron Track set; Modelkasten A-7 Detail part set for StuG IIIG; Friulmodel AW-19 Idler Wheels Panther G Late; Modeling Artisan Mori MGP14 German AFV Tools; Modeling Artisan Mori MGP15 German 20-ton Jack set; Tamiya 35173 German Panther 75mm Ammo set
Gun barrel:	Aber 35L36 Panther G late 75mm

Introduction

Beginning in March 1944, the firms assembling Panther tanks started to switch over production to the Panther Ausf. G. With the turret retained from the Ausf. A, the Ausf. G. had a redesigned hull, with the pannier sides being a single piece instead of the multipart assembly of the previous versions. Numerous other improvements were also made throughout the hull and drive train.

This model represents one of the last configurations of Panther Ausf. G that would have been produced in March/April 1945. It has specific features such as the camouflage loops on the turret sides, MG post on the cupola, *Flammenvernichter* exhausts and steel-tyred roadwheels on the last station. Period photos of this vehicle show it sitting in a vehicle dump, next to another similarly configured Panther tank, at the end of the war.

Lower hull and running gear

The Tamiya Panther Ausf. G kits are now over ten years old and lack many of the smaller details that have been discovered by research conducted over the last few years. Also many of the fittings on the lower hull are simplified and the roadwheels lack the distinctive tyre bulge around the rim. This was added to the Tamiya wheels using 0.25mm styrene rod, after it was first curled by pulling it across an X-Acto blade and then slowly glued to the kit wheel. Once the glue was dry I blended the outer surface of the rod into the wheel with a No. 11 blade as it was slowly turned in a drill. The rear lower hull side extensions were corrected as they are incorrectly shaped and have the clevis-mounting hole in the wrong position. A pair of masters was made from styrene and copies cast for use on the kit.

To prepare the kit for the addition of an interior, all of the mounting points for the roadwheel arms were removed from the inside of the lower hull using a Dremel tool. At the same time, I cut down the part of the arm that would be inserted into the lower hull, as this area would eventually be filled with internal torsion bar detail.

The vehicle I was modelling needed to have a set of steel-tyred wheels on the last station of each side. Unfortunately the steel-tyred wheels that Tamiya provides with kit number 35176 are not the correct size, as they are the same diameter as the rubber-tyred wheels. Instead they should be approximately 23mm in diameter. Rather than purchase a DML kit to pilfer the wheels from, I scratch built them.

Tamiya's Panther Ausf. G kit was built as an April 1945, MAN-production vehicle.

Upper hull and turret

The upper glacis plate in the Tamiya kit has its top corner sitting too high: it should only be about 0.5mm above the hull roof. To correct this detail I first removed the rotating periscope housing with an etched razor saw. The periscope housing needs to be moved forward by 0.5mm once the glacis has been corrected. After marking the new location for the top of the glacis I carefully scraped back the plastic with a new No. 11 blade, ensuring the blade remained perpendicular to the face of the plate. Once the glacis edge was in the correct spot, the material just in front of the forwardmost roof plate was removed so 0.5mm square styrene strip could be added. This styrene needs to be added so that the front edge of this plate is moved forward. A new weld bead was then created between this plate and front glacis using Apoxie Clay.

Tamiya's trunnion housing is about 1mm too narrow and doesn't line up properly to the front turret plate. Using a razor saw I cut apart the trunnion housing at one end then added a 1mm-thick piece of styrene, which was then filed smooth to match the existing profile of the kit part. The joint between the trunnion housing and the turret front plate was smoothed out with Apoxie Clay and the parts were given a cast texture with Mr Surfacer 500.

With all the interior detail that was going to be added to the kit, I wanted to have all the hatches removable for viewing. I decided it would be easier to entirely replace the kit's hull roof with styrene and then remove the hatches from the kit

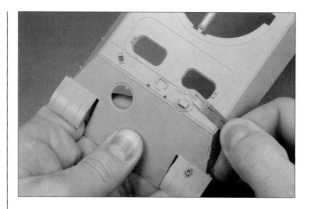

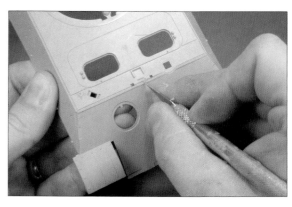

The driver's rotating periscope mechanism was removed with a thin razor saw in preparation for correcting the glacis plate and hull roof joint.

The kit plastic is carefully scraped back to the pencil line that marks the correct top of glacis edge.

The front edge of the forward top deck plate needs to be moved forward. This was done by gluing in a piece of 0.5mm square styrene.

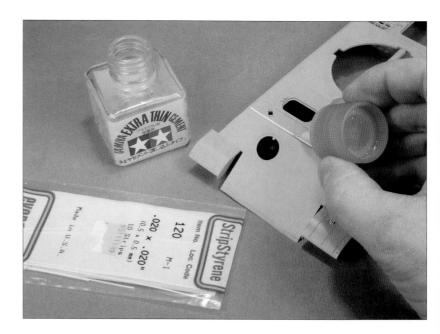

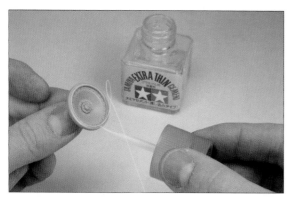

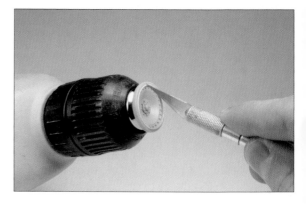

Tamiya's outermost roadwheels are missing the distinctive bulge in the rubber adjacent to the steel rim of the wheel. This was added with 0.25mm styrene rod.

Once the glue had dried the styrene rod was blended into the tyre, with a No. 11 X-Acto blade, while turning in a drill.

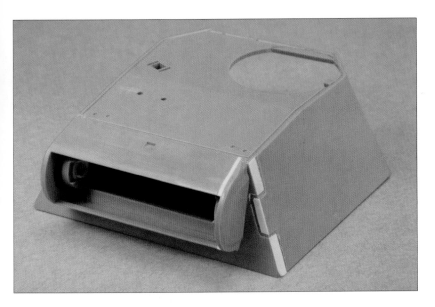

The trunnion housing in the Tamiya kit was widened by 1mm so it would properly line up with the front plate of the turret.

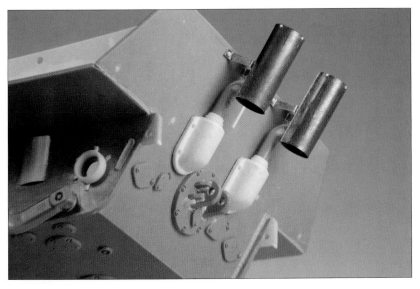

The rear hull side extensions in the kit are incorrectly shaped and have the towing clevis hole in the wrong position. Replacements were cast from a master made from styrene.

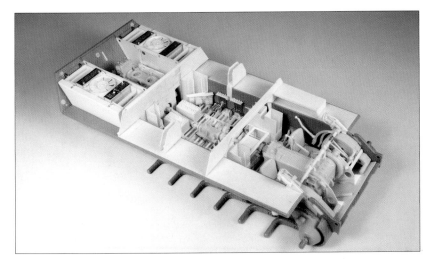

During the construction of the interior constant test fitting of parts was required. This ensured a good fit between the CMK and scratch-built items.

Included in the CMK engine set (3028) is an excellent rendition of the Maybach HL 230 P30 engine.

Cooling fan and radiator assemblies were scratch built as the CMK set included 16-blade fans instead of ones with eight blades for a late Panther G.

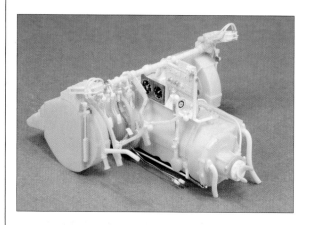

In October 1944 elevated seats started to be installed for the driver; this required extended driving controls and a new instrument panel. These components are missing from the CMK interior so they were made from styrene.

The welded armoured guard for the exhaust fan was taken from the DML Panther Ausf. A Late kit.

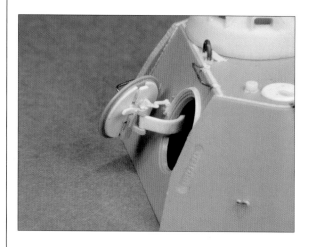

The missing hinge and locking elements of the turret's rear hatch were scratch built from styrene.

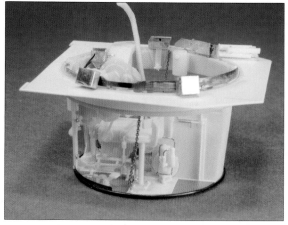

The turret set from CMK is fairly complete with just a few missing items added: some wiring, compressor elements, coaxial expended-round collector and flip-down step for the gunner.

ABOVE Inside the turret, a *Nahverteidigungswaffe* (close-defence weapon) was mounted in the rear right-hand side of the turret roof.

LEFT The tops of each radiator were thin-gauge aluminium embossed over a styrene form.

With the introduction of the crew compartment heater, changes were made to the configuration of the firewall.

part. This also allowed me to remove one of the rectangular engine deck grilles and correct its shape, as it's missing two web-shaped protrusions on one end. A mould of this part was then made and four copies cast for use on the model.

Interior

My original plan was to use all three of the interior details sets produced by CMK of the Czech Republic for Tamiya's Panther G kit. Though well cast and nicely detailed many of the parts are incorrect for the interior of a Panther Ausf. G, being more accurate for a Panther Ausf. A. I was only able to use about 25 per cent of the parts in any of the sets with the rest having to be scratch built from styrene. All parts that could be used were cleaned up, taking care not to create too much resin dust, and set aside.

The first area I tackled was a new floor insert with torsion bar detail. The CMK set has the torsion bars moulded integral with the floor and I wanted to show the numerous pipes and hoses running under the bars. Masters were made for each end of the torsion bar rods and copies cast. To represent the rods themselves I used 1mm styrene rod that was inserted at each end into the castings. Once the torsion bars were all in place I could now use the spacing of them, when compared to actual photos, to calculate the positions of the other parts.

The radiator and fan housings provided in the CMK set are not the correct configuration for a Panther G, as they have 16 fan blades instead of eight. They also have the incorrect number of fins on the air inlets at each of the radiators. New housings and fans were scratch built using photos that I had taken of actual housings as a guide. The size and shape of these were calculated based on the dimensions of the Tamiya kit engine deck and the fit double-checked with CMK's resin engine. Once these parts had been built, I made new engine bay sides and fuel tanks to fit around them. Miscellaneous hoses and fittings missing from the CMK set were made from styrene tubing.

Extended driver's controls were made from styrene and added to the transmission, as these were mounted starting in October 1944 when the elevated driver's seat was introduced. A new instrument panel was also made from styrene because this part changed at the same time as the introduction of the elevated seat, and CMK provides the earlier version.

Photo-etching

The interior ammunition stowage in the Panther Ausf. G was quite different from that of the Ausf. A and again the CMK set includes the Ausf. A configuration. The number of rounds and shape of the stowage bins were completely different so new bins were made from styrene and the sponson ammo racks were custom etched. The etched ammo rack arms were first 'modelled' in 3D using a computer program

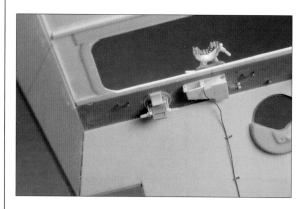

The driver's rotating periscope mount and front vent were scratch built from sheet styrene and rod.

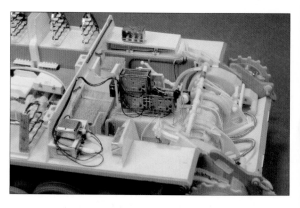

Aber's excellent multipart photo-etched Fu.2 and Fu.5 radio set was used in place of the single-piece CMK casting.

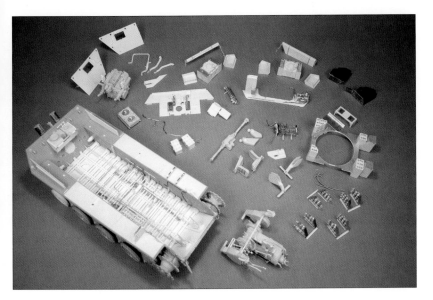

The majority of the interior components were removed in preparation for painting.

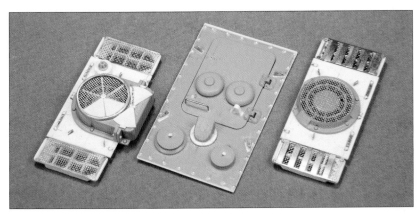

The four rectangular grilles were cast from a master that was made by correcting Tamiya's kit part.

called SolidWorks. These arms were 'modelled' at the same thickness as the brass I was using; this allowed me to create 2D 'flats' for each of the pieces. These 'flats' were then brought into AutoCAD and orientated together and a frame drawn around them. Using my inkjet printer and special clear etch film, available from Micro Mark, I created two negatives that could be used with pre-treated photosensitive brass sheets. These brass sheets were then subjected to UV rays with the negatives placed on both sides. The clear areas of the negative allow the photo-resist material to harden, which protects the brass during etching. These brass sheets were then dipped in a sodium hydroxide solution that removed the unprotected photo-resist material. Next the brass was placed in a container of ferric chloride, which ate away the unprotected brass. Once the parts were cleaned up and removed from the carrier frame the small spring-loaded clasps that connected the racks together were made from styrene.

When the crew compartment heater was introduced the configuration of the firewall changed as some items had to be removed and others relocated to accommodate the duct inlets. The CMK set provides the configuration of firewall prior to the introduction of the heater so a new one was made from styrene. This was one of the more difficult items to build, as I do not know of any complete photo coverage of this area. All of my references only partially showed areas of the firewall, especially where the duct inlets were located. By combining the various pictures and with some educated guesswork, I was able to piece together a fairly good representation.

Supplied in the CMK set is a one-piece casting of the radio set mounted in the Panther tank and, while well detailed, I decided to make my life a little tougher and use the Aber multipart etched radio set. The number of parts included in this set is staggering with numerous smaller radio components included. It took several evenings just to put everything together and wire it all up. Thankfully Aber provided a wiring diagram along with the instructions for building the parts.

The larger parts supplied in the CMK turret set were used with the majority of the smaller items scratch built from styrene, such as the parts on the underside of the turret roof. A few items were missing from the set, such as the small cylinders on the compressor, hinged step for the gunner and the removable bin for collecting the expended coaxial machine-gun rounds. Cabling and wires were also added using various gauges of copper and brass wire.

Throughout the construction of the interior, constant test fitting of parts was required to make sure everything would fit together properly. I also left as many items as I could removable, to make painting the interior easier. To ensure that these parts would line up properly during each test fit, small locating features were added where required.

Interior painting

With the majority of the interior removed in preparation for painting, I painted the entire lower hull and engine bay parts with Floquil Flat Black. Over this I started filling in the main colour of Floquil Red Oxide, leaving areas of the black showing through in the recessed areas. The torsion bars were painted with Humbrol Metal-Cote Gunmetal (27004), which was then buffed to a light metallic sheen. The housings at the ends of the torsion bars were painted with Testors' Aluminium (1181) then overpainted with Tamiya Smoke (X-19); this gives them a slightly oily look.

The assembled engine was also painted flat black with various shades of grey and silver used to pick out details. Before the engine bay was installed it was weathered with oil paints and given some light paint chipping, which was picked out with Vallejo Model Color paints. The main body of the radiator and fan housing was painted with a flat aluminium colour that had a little flat white mixed in. These were then drybrushed with an unaltered aluminium colour to pick out the highlights. After painting the tops of the radiators flat black, paint chipping was added with a dark grey colour. The fuel tanks

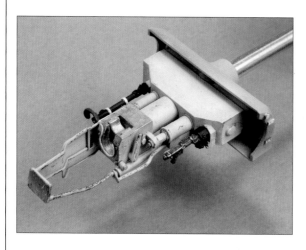

After painting the breech face and top with Testors' Aluminium (1181) it was overpainted with Tamiya Smoke (X-19) to give it an oily appearance.

Once the turret basket was painted it received localized heavy washes of thinned burnt umber oil paint. This was then followed by an application of earth-coloured pigments on the treadplate floor.

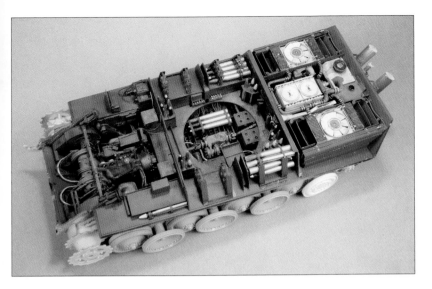

In April 1945 the main interior colour, excluding turrets, of German Panzers would have been red oxide primer.

The aluminium portion of the fan radiator assemblies was painted with Tamiya Flat Aluminium (XF-16) mixed with a little Flat White (XF-2). This was then lightly drybrushed with Testors' Aluminium (1181).

Light paint chipping of the transmission and instrument panels was done using Vallejo Dark Blue Grey (904).

Ammo stowage in the Panther Ausf. G was increased to 82 rounds for the main gun, up from 79 in Ausf. D and A.

Three sets of Tamiya's brass-turned Panther ammo were used. The majority of the ammunition had the casing portion painted with Testors' Aluminium (1181). This was then sprayed with a mixture of Tamiya Smoke (X-19) mixed with Clear Green (X-25).

Each of the Aber radio units was painted a slightly different colour.

mounted adjacent to the radiators were painted a red oxide colour and finished off with dark grey hoses; some light fuel stains were added with thinned Tamiya Smoke (X-19) and Clear Orange (X-26).

At the front of the vehicle the transmission was painted a blue grey colour mixed from Tamiya acrylic paints. It was treated to some light paint chipping using Vallejo Dark Blue Grey (904) and a fine-tipped paintbrush. I had previously masked the dials with Vallejo Liquid Mask and this was now removed with a toothpick. Each of the Aber radio units was painted a slightly different shade of dark grey to reinforce that they were separate components. Labels for the dials and knobs were painted with Vallejo Model Color paints. The cords running to the dynamotors were painted a dark grey colour while the interconnecting wires were painted a dark brown colour.

Throughout the lower interior light paint chipping was added to areas that would be subject wear from the crew, picked out with Vallejo Hull Red (985). This colour was lightened and darkened throughout its use, which imparted a more random nature to the chips. As a final touch, the same areas of the interior were lightly drybrushed with Humbrol Metal-Cote Gunmetal (27004).

The interior of the turret was also painted with Floquil Flat Black as a base colour over which I carefully applied an off-white mixture of Vallejo Model Air White (001) mixed with a little Sand (075). Weathering of the turret interior and turntable was carried out in much the same way as the lower hull, with shades of the primer and an ivory colour applied as paint chips throughout. The face and top of the breech were painted with Testors' Aluminium (1181) and then overpainted with Tamiya Smoke (X-19) to give them an oily appearance.

Exterior detailing

With the interior finished the upper hull was glued to the lower and the remaining weld beads were added using Apoxie Clay. The etched tool racks are from the Aber set for the Panther G (35024); however, rather than use the clasps supplied in that set I replaced them with ones from a separate Aber clasp set (35A93). This newer set provides clasps that are closer to scale than the older Aber items. Equipping the tool racks are items from Modelling Artisan Mori's German AFV tools (MGP14) and German 20-ton Jack set (MGP15). The stowage bins mounted on the rear of the hull are also from Aber and were soldered together as previously described.

The two outer engine deck plates, with the circular grilles, were made from 0.5mm styrene to which grilles and my resin castings were added. Screens from the Aber Panther set were added with the sliding louvres taken from the new Aber set for late model Panther Gs (35G14).

Numerous items such as the cylindrical stowage bin, clamps for poison gas-detection cards, mount for the *Ostercompass* and the hood over the driver's periscope were made from thin-gauge aluminium sheet. Most of these items are provided in the Aber etch set but they are either too small or incorrect.

Painting the exterior

After masking all the openings the model was primed light grey, pre-shaded with flat black and then basecoated with Vallejo Model Air Panzer Olive Green 1943 (096). This was left to dry for 24 hours during which time I created the masks that would be used to aid in painting the hard-edge camouflage scheme. I first planned out the scheme on another Tamiya kit, over which I applied sections of a grocery bag that had a low tack adhesive applied to one side. The patterns were then traced onto the sections of bag, which were then removed and cut apart along the lines. These were then re-applied to the model and the camouflage colour applied using a combination of Vallejo Model Air Dark Yellow (025) lightened with Sand (075), mixed at a 3:1 ratio. The model was weathered as described in previous chapters.

The Panther G lower hull no longer had the interlocking wedge-shaped sponson sides. Instead the superstructure was one single plate. This change simplified production.

WWII Productions' resin track links were used on the kit. These links require minimal cleanup and simply snap together.

The Panther Ausf. G no longer had the driver's visor mounted in the glacis plate. Instead a pivoting, traversable periscope was mounted in the fore hull roof.

An overview of the completed construction phase.

In preparation for painting of the hard-edge camouflage, the base colour was masked off using Krylon Easy-Tack applied to pieces of a plastic grocery bag.

Vallejo Model Air Dark Yellow (025) and Sand (075) were mixed together and sprayed onto the model at approximately 15psi.

The five semicircular loops on each side of the turret were for attaching camouflage.

ABOVE **MIG** Productions' pigments were applied to the lower tracks and hull.

BELOW The driver's and radio operator's hatches were supported when opening and closing by small rollers, mounted on spring-loaded arms.

ABOVE **Humbrol Metal-Cote Gunmetal (27004) was sparingly drybrushed around crew entry/exit points. Once buffed this gives a nice lightly polished steel appearance.**

BELOW **All access plates and the turret were left removable so the interior can be viewed.**

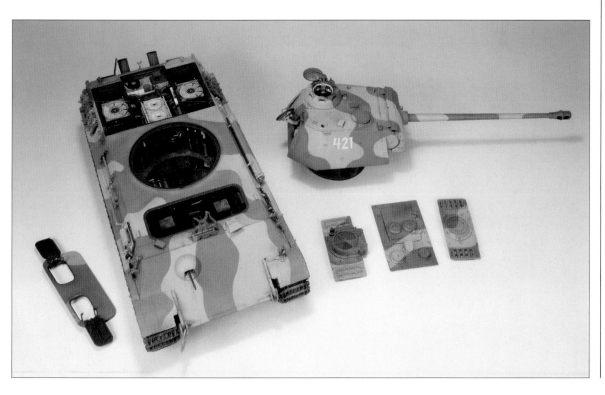

ABOVE The glass portion of the rear convoy light was first painted white, then overpainted with Tamiya Clear Blue (X-23).

BELOW It's not known why, but on several Panthers completed by MAN in March and April 1945, steel roadwheels were mounted on the last station.

Special feature – Bergepanther Ausf. A and Pantherturm

Subject:	*Bergepanther Ausf. A*
Kit used:	*DML Sd.Kfz.171 Panther A Early Type (Italy 1943/44) kit number 6160*
Skill level:	*Advanced*
Resin detail sets:	*On Track Models 35005 Bergepanther G Conversion (out of production); CMK 3029 Pz.V Panther – Driver's set*
Etched-metal sets:	*Eduard 35119 - Panzer V Bergepanther; Como Models 35B001 Panther A/D Grille set (for Dragon)*
Tracks and misc. details:	*Modelkasten SK-10 Panther Late Model Track set; Modelkasten SK-15 Panther Late Model Spare Track set; Plus Model 115 – Fuel-Stock Equipment, Germany – WWII; Tiger Model Designs 351012 Chain Hoist 2; Tiger Model Designs 00010 Extra Fine Chain/42 link-per-inch*
Figure:	*Wolf Models WAW10 British Soldier*
Gun barrel:	*Fine Molds MG-45D Panther 7.5cm Gun Barrel*

Introduction

Starting in mid-1943 a small batch of 12 Bergepanthers were created on a Panther Ausf. D hull by leaving off the turret and covering the turret ring with decking. Starting in July of that same year Bergepanthers began to be produced on dedicated hulls that had large openings in the hull roof, to accommodate the large 40-ton capacity winch assembly. Surrounding the winch was a built-up superstructure called a 'bridge'. This version of the Bergepanther was produced with modifications introduced during its production run until October 1944, when the hull shape took that of the Panther Ausf. G.

The vehicle modelled in this section is one of the later versions of the second series as it has the same external tool stowage configuration as a Bergepanther Ausf. G. It is based on photos of a vehicle that was captured in Europe and sent back to England for evaluation by the 'School of Tank Technology'. A copy of the ensuing report, which was written during World War II, was used as a guide while building the model.

Lower hull and running gear

Visible in the period photographs of the vehicle I was modelling was a roughly applied section of *Zimmerit* on the lower hull sides. To replicate this pattern I used Apoxie Clay that, once mixed together, was pushed onto the lower hull and smoothed out with water. While the surface of the putty was still wet I pushed the ridges into the putty one at a time using a small piece of brass flat bar.

Due to the heavy weight of the spade assembly on the rear of the hull, the Bergepanther had a tail-down appearance. Wanting my model to have a similar look I removed all but the front roadwheel arm with a razor saw, cutting them all off in one go. Small discs of plastic, the same diameter as the arm, were glued onto the ends of the removed pieces to compensate for the material removed during the cutting process. The arms were then glued back on the lower hull

The DML Early Panther Ausf. A was converted to a Bergepanther and placed in a small scene with a Wolf Models' British Soldier.

with each one being positioned slightly higher as I moved towards the rear. To provide additional strength the last arm on each side had a short section of brass wire inserted into the end of it that lined up with a corresponding hole on the lower hull.

The welded tow bracket, engine-starter mounts and port cover were added to the engine access hatch on the rear hull. The extended rear tow coupling was scratch built using photos from the report as a guide. The assembly of the On Track spade was fairly straightforward; however, a few of the parts were slightly warped but this was easy to correct with some warm water and a little patience. Some additional details were added, such as gussets and a correctly sized tip on the end of the spade. The DML kit exhausts were extended with 2.4mm styrene tube and then covered in Mr Surfacer 500.

The interior of the lower hull was outfitted with the transmission, seats, shock absorbers, floor insert and firewall from the CMK interior set for the Tamiya Panther G. A new forward bulkhead with winch controls was made from rod and sheet styrene. I also decided to scratch build an empty radio rack over the transmission, as I figured the sets would have been removed long before the vehicle was subject to testing. The Bergepanther also had extra fuel tanks mounted in the sponsons, so these were built up from styrene and retaining straps made from aluminium sheet were added.

Upper hull and winch assembly

Rather than try and cut through the kit's thick hull roof then patch and fill the forward vent hole, I removed the entire top plate forward of the engine deck. This was done rather quickly using a cutting bit in my Dremel tool, leaving about 1mm of material all the way around. This last amount of material was then carefully filed back until the inner edges of the roof and side plate interlocking welds were reached. I then measured the finished opening and transferred these dimensions to a sheet of 0.5mm-thick styrene sheet. Using the excellent drawings in *Panzer Tracts No. 5-2* for my measurements, I also marked out the periscope openings. Referencing the report photos, the opening for the winch assembly was marked out. After cutting out all the openings the new roof was glued to the kit and any seams filled with Squadron white putty.

Provided in the On Track conversion set is a nicely detailed and well-cast winch assembly, although I did replace some of the more heavily cast items with versions made from copper sheet. Additional detailing was also done

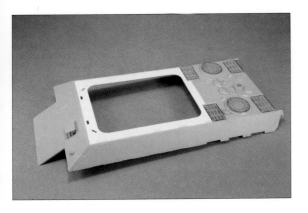

The kit roof was replaced with one made from sheet styrene.

A small styrene jig was used to ensure that added detail on the lower hull sides would be symmetrical.

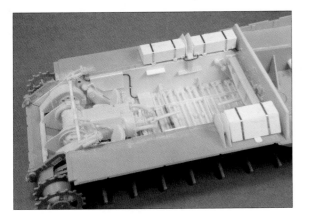

CMK's excellent Panther transmission, torsion bar inserts and firewall were used to detail the lower hull.

The lower hull sides received an application of *Zimmerit* using Apoxie Clay.

using styrene, brass tubing and aluminium sheet. The entire 'bridge' structure was completely scratch built from 0.25mm sheet styrene, this time using the drawings in *Panzer Tracts No. 16* and period photos as guides. Internal storage compartments were made using thin aluminium sheet and two small racks were made from strips of copper, so they could be soldered together.

Parts of the On Track Models jib-boom were replaced with styrene tube as they were badly warped. The base mounts for the boom on either side of the superstructure were made from bits of styrene with the weld beads created using 0.25mm styrene rod. The rod was glued around the scratch-built items and liquid glue applied until it softened. Using a No. 11 X-Acto blade small cuts and grooves were pushed into the pliable styrene creating the look of a weld bead. Finishing off the jib-boom assembly was a chain hoist from Tiger Model Designs, which is a nicely cast set that comes with lengths of small-scale chain (42 links/inch).

Painting and weathering

The interior of the model was first primed with Floquil Flat Black as a base colour over which I carefully applied an off-white mixture of Vallejo Model Air White (001) mixed with a little Sand (075) on the upper areas. After masking off the white colour the lower portion was painted Floquil Red Oxide part-way up the hull sides leaving areas of the black showing through in the recessed areas. The torsion bars were painted with Humbrol Metal-Cote Gunmetal

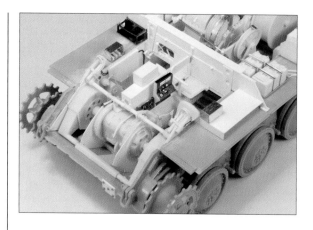

A new bulkhead behind the radio operator's and driver's seats was made from styrene, complete with winch controls.

The winch assembly from the now out-of-production On Track Models Bergepanther conversion was detailed further.

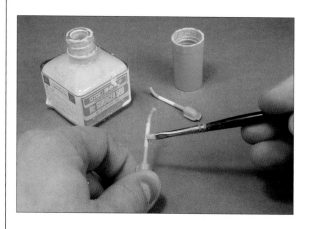

After extending the DML kit exhausts with 2.4mm styrene tube they were covered in Mr Surfacer 500.

The interior was painted and weathered prior to adding the upper hull. A heavy application of washes and pigments gave the interior a well-used look.

(27004), which was then buffed to a light metallic sheen. The transmission was painted a blue-green colour and the extra fuel tanks a dark yellow with both colours mixed from Tamiya paints. The whole interior was then given a heavy wash of Winsor & Newton Raw Umber thinned with mineral spirits. When this was dry, small amounts of pigments were dusted throughout the lower hull and the interior was then sealed up.

The winch assembly was painted a *dunkelgelb* colour mixed from Tamiya Dark Yellow (XF-60) lightened with Flat White (XF-2) at a 75 to 25 per cent ratio. It was then given a wash of thinned oil paints, and some light paint chipping picked out with dark brown colours from the Vallejo Model Color range. Supplied with the winch assembly is a piece of black nylon string that is used for the winch cable. After winding the string around the winch drum and pulleys it was sprayed with Model Master's Flat Clear to seal it. Humbrol Metal-Cote Gunmetal (27004) was then brush-painted over this and buffed slightly to give it a metallic sheen. An application of Rustall and earth-coloured pigments finished off the cable. The last section of the winch cable that would run out the backside of the bridge was left separate so that it could be added after the exterior painting was complete.

With the painting of the interior complete, the open areas were masked off and the exterior was primed with Floquil Grey Primer. The spade was then

Added to the engine access hatch in the DML Early Panther Ausf. A kit were the welded tow bracket and the engine starter mounts and port cover.

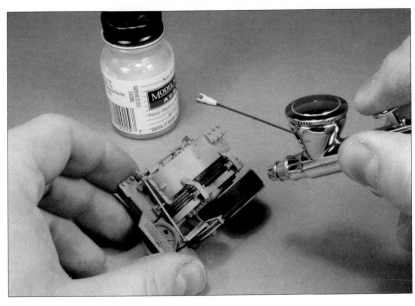

The nylon rope to be used for the winch cable was airbrushed with Model Master Clear Flat before being painted a steel colour.

painted in a dark steel colour over which I randomly applied Vallejo Liquid Mask along the rear edge. The entire model was then basecoated in a *dunkelgelb* colour using a mixture of Tamiya acrylic paints. After carefully studying the period photos of the vehicle being modelled, I made several sketches of the camouflage patterns to use as a guide during the painting process. Before painting the rear spade with the camouflage colours, it was again randomly sponged with the liquid mask. I used Tamiya Red Brown (XF-64) and Vallejo Model Air Panzer Olive Green 1943 (096) for each of the camouflage colours. Using acrylics meant I could move straight to giving the model a light wash of raw umber oil paint thinned with mineral spirits. The wash also helped lift the liquid mask from the surface of the spade, revealing a multi-layered scratched paint effect. This was further highlighted with a light drybrushing of Testors' Aluminium (1181) and some additional scratches added with the tip of a No. 11 X-Acto blade. A heavy application of paint chips was also applied over the entire model on areas that would see wear from the crew using a mixture of different Vallejo Model colours. Additional weathering was carried out as described in the previous chapters.

Due to the heavy weight of the large spade, Bergepanthers had a tail-heavy appearance. The suspension arms were removed and repositioned to replicate this look.

The extended rear tow coupling was scratch built to replicate what can be seen in photo references.

Modelkasten SK-10 Panther Late Model workable tracks were used on the kit.

Vignette base and figure

A small pre-sized and edged detailed base was purchased at a local craft store. After staining and finishing the wood, the edges were masked off with green painters' tape. The exposed area of the base was then roughened with 120-grit sandpaper to aid in the adhesion of the groundwork. The small hill at the rear corner of the base was built up using small pieces of Styrofoam, attached to the base with white glue. A combination of Sculptamold, earth-coloured craft store paints and a small amount of water was mixed together in an old plastic container. This mixture was then evenly spread out onto the base using an old spoon. While still wet, finely ground, unscented cat litter was sprinkled around the base to represent small rocks. Track marks and footprints were also added to the base before the groundwork had hardened.

On the lower part of the small hill static grass was sprinkled overtop watered-down white glue. The longer pieces of grass on the upper part of the hill were made from a basket liner that was randomly pulled apart. As this was much thicker than the previously applied static grass, white glue unaltered was used to hold it in place. To unite the different colours of the grass elements they were both lightly sprayed with a mixture of Tamiya Flat Green (XF-5) and Buff (XF-57). The groundwork was then airbrushed various shades of earth-toned colours, keeping in mind those colours used to previously weather the model. To finish off the groundwork it was randomly dusted with the same pigments used on the model.

A Wolf Models' white metal figure of a British soldier was placed on the base with the Bergepanther to represent one of the inspectors that would have examined and tested the captured vehicle back in England.

The face and hands of the figure were first primed with Tamiya Flat Flesh (XF-15) and then painted in artist's oils, using mostly White, Burnt Sienna and some Raw Umber by Winsor & Newton. Before the face had dried Payne's Grey was very lightly painted onto the lower jaw and a small amount of a light pink colour onto the lower lip. The uniform was painted with various Vallejo Model paints, as they go on beautifully leaving no brush marks. Once the figure had been attached to the base the same earth-coloured pigments used on the base were dabbed around the figure's feet to bring continuity to the scene.

The 'bridge' superstructure was made from 0.25mm styrene sheet. Small-scale chain (42 links/inch) from Tiger Model Designs was used on the fold-down sides.

A mixture of Sculptamold, Hudson and Allen Muck, white glue and earth-coloured craft paints was spread onto the base.

Finely ground, unscented cat litter was sprinkled around the base to represent small rocks.

Static grass and strands pulled from a basket liner set were used to create the small grassy patch on the base. To unite the different colours of the grass elements they were both lightly sprayed with a mixture of Tamiya Flat Green (XF-5) and Buff (XF-57).

To create a continuity between the figure, model and base the same pigments were applied to each.

Track impressions on the base were made using an old Tamiya Jagdpanther kit, prior to the groundwork hardening.

The large spade was painted in several layers with each layer having portions of the paint masked with Vallejo Liquid Mask (523).

Specific details such as the broken wire step and push plate, missing headlight and the glacis markings were all replicated from photos of the actual vehicle.

Tiger Model Design's Chain Hoist No. 2 (351012) was used with parts from the On-Track conversion.

The 'bridge' area of the model was heavily weathered using a combination of Vallejo Liquid Mask (523) and post-applied paint chips.

Two additional crew seats were mounted behind the existing radio operator's and driver's seats.

Using photos of the actual vehicle as a guide, oil leaks and stains were added to the various ports on the rear hull.

Pantherturm

In late 1943 Panther turrets, mounted over fixed structures, started to be used as gun emplacements, called Pantherturms. These were basically lower chambers, consisting of living quarters and ammo storage, constructed either of wood, steel or concrete over which a Panther turret was mounted. A specifically manufactured turret was mounted over the lower chambers but sometimes production turrets were also used.

With the leftover turret from the Bergepanther conversion I was able to build a small scene depicting a Pantherturm being installed. I chose to model a version that had the lower chambers manufactured from steel. The lower structures were scratch built from 0.5mm thick styrene sheet, which had 1.5mm square rod glued around the perimeter. This way I was able to give the impression of heavy steel plates without having to use a lot of styrene.

The DML turret was assembled as per the kit instructions with the only alterations being the addition of a Fine Molds' aluminium barrel (MG-45D) and some cast texture added, with Mr Surfacer 500, to the cupola and front plate.

The lower structure interior was painted with Tamiya Flat Black (XF-1) as a base colour over which I carefully applied Floquil Red Oxide, leaving small areas of the black showing through. The opening was then masked off and the exterior primed Floquil Grey Primer over which I again applied the red oxide colour.

The assembled turret was also first painted with Floquil Grey Primer, then painted a *dunkelgelb* colour mixed from Tamiya Dark Yellow (XF-60) lightened with Flat White (XF-2) at a 75 to 25 per cent ratio. A lightly applied single camouflage colour was applied using Vallejo Model Air Tank Green (011).

Used as fixed fortifications some production Panther Ausf. A turrets were mounted on steel structures, called *O.T.-Stahlunterstands*, in Italy.

The Pantherturm structure was constructed so that it could be taken apart for painting.

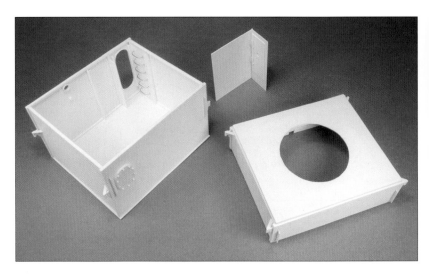

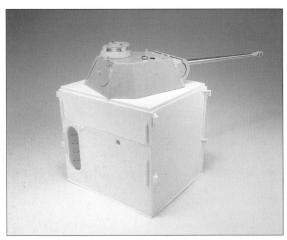

The turret from DML's Early Panther Ausf. A, left over from the Bergepanther conversion, was mounted on the scratch-built Pantherturm structure.

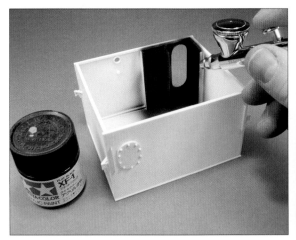

The interior of the structure was first painted Tamiya Flat Black (XF-I) over which the red oxide colour was applied.

Floquil Red Oxide enamel was used for the overall colour of the Pantherturm structure.

A single camouflage scheme was applied using Vallejo Model Air Tank Green (011).

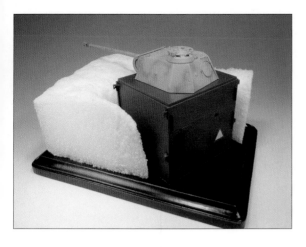

Before applying the groundwork the model was test fitted to ensure there was adequate room around the structure.

Polyfilla and various craft store paints were mixed with water to create the groundwork. The base has been masked off with painter's tape.

By increasing the amount of dry Polyfilla mixed with water a lumpier and grainer mixture was achieved.

The text inside the red-bordered triangles was applied via a custom decal, made on my inkjet printer.

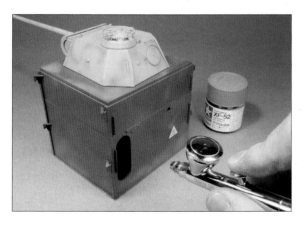

Tamiya Flat Earth (XF-52) was randomly applied around the structure.

Model Master Clear Gloss was applied over the Tamiya Flat Black (XF-1) on the side panels of the base.

Weldbond adhesive was used to attach the lower Pantherturm structure to the base.

The groundwork received numerous washes of burnt umber oil paint mixed with mineral spirits along with several applications of pigments.

The small dip in the side panel of the base was made so that detail on the front of the Pantherturm could still be easily viewed.

The hole to the above right of the crew entrance was for attaching a small stovepipe.

The red-bordered triangles on the front and back of the lower structure were created by first painting a solid white colour through a custom-made stencil. A smaller triangle was then placed in the centre of the white painted area with the other stencil still in place and the red colour was applied. When both stencils were removed there was a white triangle with a red border. The text inside the triangles was made by first printing them out onto clear decal film, using an inkjet printer. To protect the ink from running when the decal gets wet it was coated with Krylon Kristal Klear. Once the decals had been applied to the model it was given a light coating of Polly Scale Satin Finish.

The groundwork on the base was built up using Styrofoam with the exposed sides covered with 0.75mm sheet styrene. With the base protected by green painter's tape a mixture of Polyfilla, craft store paints, white glue and water was applied over the Styrofoam. Once the base was entirely covered I slowly started adding dry Polyfilla into the previous wet mixture, creating a lumpier and grainier texture. This was then loosely spread around the upper edges of the Pantherturm depression. When dry the lumpy areas of the base were treated to an application of diluted white glue, to secure everything in place.

Tamiya Flat Earth (XF-52) and Buff (XF-57) were randomly sprayed over the groundwork and Pantherturm structure. This was then followed by an application of earth-coloured pigments tying everything together. Weldbond glue was used to adhere the structure to the base. Finishing things off was an application of Tamiya Flat Black around the sides followed by Model Master Clear Gloss.

Gallery

LEFT Tamiya's Panther Ausf. G kit was used to depict an actual vehicle that had been captured in Normandy and evaluated by the Allied forces. (Photo and model by David Parker)

BELOW The model features *Zimmerit* made from Milliput, a two-part epoxy putty. It also has extra detailing in the form of stowage bins made from pewter sheet, Artisan Mori resin cupola and drive sprockets along with an Aber aluminium barrel and photo-etch detail set. (Photo and model by David Parker)

ABOVE Knocked out Panzerkampfwagen V Panther Ausf. A, Normandy, 1944. This started life as the DML kit. Sam added a fully destroyed interior, burnt-out wheels, and damaged external fittings. (Photo and model by Sam Dwyer)

BELOW The engine deck has remnants of the original camouflage pattern but most of this area has been painted to show signs of internal fuel/ammo fire. (Photo and model by Sam Dwyer)

ABOVE Using DML's Panther Ausf. A Early kit and some minor
scratch building, David modelled a Befehls-Panther serving on the
Eastern Front. Aber's photo-etch set for the Italeri kit was used
for extra detailing with some parts of the set being modified to
fit the DML kit. (Photo and model by David Parker)

BELOW The model was finished in a scheme of whitewash
over a standard three-colour camouflage. Painting was done using
enamel sand for the base colour over which gouache camouflage
colours were applied. The winter whitewash was then effectively
reproduced using a combination of sprayed and brushed-on
paints. (Photo and model by David Parker)

ABOVE Bergepanther Ausf. A constructed from the DML Early A Panther and converted by Sam Dwyer, using CMK's driver's interior, On Track Models' Bergepanther conversion, and a lot of scratch building. (Photo and model by Sam Dwyer)

BELOW Looking into the winch compartment. The On Track Models' winch was replaced with the Verlinden Productions' winch, mainly because of so many missing parts in the OTM kit. (Photo and model by Sam Dwyer)

LEFT This model was finished in 2002 and depicts an early Panther G tank of the 4th company of SS-Panzer Regiment 12 in Normandy in early June 1944. The Tamiya 1/35-scale Panther G Frühe kit was the basis, with many modifications and Aber photo-etched parts. The front fenders, storage tube and rear bins were made from foil. The *Zimmerit* was made from two-part epoxy and was patterned with a watch crown. (Photo and model by Manus Gallagher)

BELOW The resin tracks were made by the now-defunct Anvil Miniatures and the figure was a modified Dragon US Tanker body with a head from their Hummel crew set. Tamiya acrylic paints were used with Humbrol enamels for the turret numbers, weathering and other details. (Photo and model by Manus Gallagher)

Museums and collections

Musée des Blindés (Saumur, France)
Both a Panther Ausf. A and Bergepanther Ausf. G reside at this museum. The Panther Ausf. A is in running condition and the Bergepanther has its winch mechanism removed for better viewing.

Oorlogs en Verzets Museum (Overloon, The Netherlands)
An early version of the Panther Ausf. G is on display at this museum, which has partially restored the exterior. Unfortunately many of the restored components, including the *Zimmerit*, are inaccurate for a wartime vehicle.

The town of Breda (The Netherlands)
On display is a Panther Ausf. D, which was presented to the town by Polish forces at the end of World War II. This vehicle has the asymmetrical grilles present on the early version of the Ausf. D.

The town of Houffalize (Belgium)
On display in this small town, which is about 16km from Bastogne, is an early-version Panther Ausf. G that was lost during the Battle of the Bulge. This vehicle was produced sometime before July 1944 as it has the square cut in the glacis plate for the driver's periscope.

Worthington Memorial Park Armor Museum (Camp Borden, Canada)
This open-air museum, located on one of Canada's Armed Forces bases, has a Panther Ausf. A on display.

Military Vehicle Technology Foundation (California, USA)
This museum recently acquired a Panther Ausf. A hull and turret from somewhere in Eastern Europe. They are currently undergoing restoration with the intent to make a complete vehicle and bring it back to running condition.

Koblenz Army Museum (Germany)
A late Panther Ausf. G, manufactured post war, is on display at this museum. It has most of the features of a Panther produced in January or February of 1945, such as no MG ring on the cast cupola, and half the engine deck mounting bolts. Unfortunately the museum has added *Zimmerit* to this vehicle, which isn't accurate given its other features.

Patton Museum (Fort Knox, USA)
Sitting on display outdoors is a Panther Ausf. G. This example has a turret that contains the semicircular camouflage rings that were added starting in March 1945. Strangely this vehicle's hull is sitting much higher than normal. Luckily, this allows detail normally hidden by the wheels to be well seen.

Aberdeen Proving Grounds (Maryland, USA)
This large, mainly outdoor, museum has two different version of the Panther tank, an Ausf. A and Ausf. G.

The Tank Museum Bovington (Dorset, England)
Housed in this museum is a Panther Ausf. G that was produced post war, under REME supervision, by a team of former MNH workers.

The Panther Ausf. G at Aberdeen Proving Grounds in Maryland, USA.

Further reading, media and websites

Books

Achtung Panzer No. 4, Dai Nippon Kaiga: Tokyo, 1994
This is an excellent book for the modeller to have as it contains plenty of information about the Panther tank and changes that occurred during production.

Cockle, Tom, *Panzers in Italy*, Concord Publications: Hong Kong, 2003
This book is a great source of photos for Panthers in service in the Italian Theatre.

Guglielmi, Daniele, *Panzer in Italy*, Publimodel: Taranto, 2001
This book is another excellent source for pictures of both Panthers and Pantherturms in the Italian Theatre.

Jentz, Thomas L., and Doyle, Hilary, *Germany's Panther Tank – The Quest for Combat Supremacy*, Schiffer Publishing Ltd: Atglen, PA, 1995
This book is considered to be the Bible of the Panther tank. It clearly describes the development of the Panther as well as chronologically depicting the modifications that occurred during production.

Jentz, Thomas L., and Doyle, Hilary, *New Vanguard 22: Panther Variants 1942–45*, Osprey Publishing Ltd: Oxford, 1997
This book is basically a condensed version of *The Quest* with the addition of information on other Panther variants.

Jentz, Thomas L., and Doyle, Hilary, *Panzer Tracts No. 16 – Bergepanzerwagen*, Darlington Productions Inc.: Darlington, MD, 1997
This is an excellent book on recovery vehicles, with a brief section on the Bergepanther. Luckily the few pages in this book contain a wealth of information on the changes that occurred during the Bergepanther's production run.

Jentz, Thomas L., and Doyle, Hilary, *Panzer Tracts No.5-1 – Panzerkampfwagen 'Panther' Ausfuehrung D*, Panzer Tracts: Boyds, MD, 2003
This booklet is a recent follow-up to Mr Jentz's previous books on the Panther. It includes the latest information that the author has uncovered in regards to the Panther Ausf. A. Included are numerous CAD drawings and photos to convey this information to the reader.

Jentz, Thomas L., and Doyle, Hilary, *Panzer Tracts No.5-2 – Panzerkampfwagen 'Panther' Ausfuehrung A*, Panzer Tracts: Boyds, MD, 2003
This is also a follow-up to *The Quest* however this booklet focuses on the second-production version of the Panther. It has the same excellent and clearly presented information as 5-1.

Jentz, Thomas L., and Doyle, Hilary, *Panzer Tracts No.5-3 – Panzerkampfwagen 'Panther' Ausfuehrung G*, Panzer Tracts: Boyds, MD, 2004
This book is the last in the Panther series and is also a follow-up to *The Quest*. It includes the latest discoveries regarding Panther Ausf. G production. It has the same presentation format as the other Panzer Tracts books.

Jentz, Thomas L., and Doyle, Hilary, *Panzer Tracts No. 21-2 – Pantherturm I und II*, Panzer Tracts: Boyds, MD, 2006
This small booklet is a comprehensive guide to the construction and employment of Pantherturm structures.

Panther at Kursk, Frontline Illustration: Russia, 2002
The issue of this Russian publication is focused on the use of the Panther during Operation *Zitadelle*. Unfortunately the text is mostly in Russian with only the picture captions in English. It does, however, contain numerous photos of the Panther both in combat and knocked out.

Panzers in Saumur No. 2, Dai Nippon Kaiga: Tokyo, 1990
In this book there are very good detail pictures of both the interior and exterior of the Panther A that resides at the Saumur museum.

Panzerwrecks 1, Panzerwrecks: Monroe, New York, 2004
This title is filled entirely with photos of knocked-out or abandoned German vehicles. It features several pictures of the modified Panthers in service with I.Abteilung/Panzer Regiment 4 in Italy.

PzKpfw. V Panther Vol. 6, Waldemar Trojca: Gdansk, 2003
This volume of the Panther series includes information on the Panther Ausf. A and the Panther Ostwallturms. It contains numerous photos and line drawings showing the different features on each of the subjects.

Spielberger, Walter J., *Panther and its Variants*, Schiffer Publishing Ltd: Atglen, PA, 1993
An excellent title on the Panther, this one includes information on the different variants of the tank. It covers those that actually entered production and ones that only made it to the drawing board.

Magazines

AFV Modeller issue 16, May/ June 2004
  This entire issue is filled with models featuring the different versions of Panther tank.
Parker, David, 'Pink Panther', *AFV Modeller* issue 4, May/June 2002
  Detailed build of DML Panther Ausf. A Early.

Websites

http://www.tankmuseum.org/
  This website doesn't contain much in the way of specific vehicle information. It does, however, contain the contact information for the museum's library, where information can be obtained.
http://www.achtungpanzer.com/
  Has a very comprehensive web page devoted to the Panther tank.
http://www.missing-lynx.com/
  An excellent website devoted to armour modelling with a gallery section that contains numerous pictures of Panther models. It also has a great discussion group section where modellers can share and discuss information.
http://www.track-link.net/
  This is one of the first websites devoted to armour modelling that I found on the Internet when I got back into the hobby. It contains numerous product reviews that are written by site users. There is also a newsgroup section and a fairly large image library containing photos of preserved museum vehicles.
http://www.ww2modelmaker.com/
  This is another excellent website that contains both newsgroups and a model gallery; it also includes a nice reference photo section. These reference photos are both period 'in action' and contemporary pictures of museum vehicles.
http://www.battlefield.ru/
  The main content of this website is the development of Soviet armour; however, there is a section on destroyed Axis tanks. In this section can be found almost two-dozen pictures of knocked-out Panthers.

Available kits and accessories in 1/35 scale

Injection-moulded kits
Panther Ausf. D
Dragon Panther Ausf. D 'Kursk, 1943' Medium Tank
No. 6164
ICM Pz.Kpfw.V Panther Ausf. D No. 35361

Panther Ausf. A
Dragon Panther Ausf. A Medium Tank (Early Type)
No. 6160
Dragon German Panther A Medium Tank (Late Type)
No. 6168
Italeri PzKpfw.V Panther Ausf. A Medium Tank
No. 270
Tamiya PzKpfw.V Panther Ausf. A Medium Tank
No. 35065

Panther Ausf. G
Tamiya PzKpfw.V Panther Ausf. G Early Version
No. 35170
Tamiya German Panther Ausf. G – Steel Wheel
Version No. 35174
Tamiya Panther Ausf. G Late Version Medium Tank
No. 35176
Tamiya Panther Ausf. G Medium Tank with *Zimmerit*
No. 35261
Dragon Panther Ausf. G 'Night Fighting' Medium
Tank No. 9045
Dragon Pz.Beob.Wg V Ausf. G Command Vehicle
No. 9041
Dragon Pz.Bfwg. Panther Ausf. G Medium Tank
No. 9046

Bergepanther
ICM Bergepanther WWII German ARV, Early Version
No. 35341
ICM Bergepanther ARV (Varly) w/Crew No. 35342

Pantherturm
Just Plane Stuff Pantherturm I No. JPS020
MIG Productions Panther Pillbox No. RW.35-013
MIG Productions Panther Pillbox Berlin
No. RW.35-014

Photo-etch detail sets
Aber Panther Ausf. A (Italeri) No. 35006
Aber Panther Ausf. G (Tamiya) No. 35024
Aber Panther Ausf. D (Italeri) No. 35029
Aber Side Skirts for Panther Ausf. A, D (Italeri)
No. 35A08
Aber Side Skirts for Panther A & D (Dragon)
No. 35A107
Aber Front Fenders for Panther Ausf. G (Tamiya)
No. 35A24
Aber Front Fenders for Panther Ausf.
A/D No. 35A31
Aber Panther – Rear Boxes No. 35A91
Aber Panther A/D Superset No. 35K02
Aber Panther Ausf. A/D Grilles No. 35G01
Aber Panther Ausf. G/F Grilles No. 35G02
Aber grilles for Panther Ausf. A/D No. 35G10
Aber grilles for Panther G (Late) No. 35G14
Aber Front Mudguards for Panther G/F &
Jagdpanther No. 35R04

Tamiya's Panther Ausf. G kit was released in 1994 and, though it suffers from a few inaccuracies, is still a nice kit.

DML's release of the Panther Ausf. D was a huge improvement over Italeri's attempt.

Sd.Kfz.171 Panther D
52nd Battalion, 39th Panzer Regiment
Kursk Offensive, July 1943
1:35 '39-'45 SERIES

DRAGON

Armorscale *Schürzen* for Pz.Kpfw.V Panther Ausf. D and A No. P35-006

Armorscale Panther Ausf. G Late engine reticular shields (Tamiya) No. P35-005

Eduard Panzer V Bergepanther No. 35119

Eduard PzBefWg. Panther Ausf. G (Dragon) No. 35255

Eduard Pz.V Panther G Early (Tamiya) No. 35354

Eduard Pz.V Panther Late (Tamiya) No. 35362

Eduard Panther G Late *Zimmerit* (Tamiya) No. 35373

Eduard Panther G Early *Zimmerit* Horizontal (Tamiya) No. 35393

Eduard Panther Ausf. A (Tamiya) No. 35424

Eduard Panther Ausf. A *Zimmerit* (Tamiya) No. 35425

Eduard Panther Ausf. A *Schürzen* – Tamiya No. 35443

Eduard Sd.Kfz.171 Panther A Early (Dragon) No. 35486

Eduard Panther A Early *Zimmerit* (Dragon) No. 35487

Eduard Panther A *Schürzen* (Dragon) No. 35501

Eduard Panther D (Dragon) No. 35505

Eduard Panther Ausf. D *Schürzen* (Dragon) No. 35513

Eduard Panther A (Dragon) No. 35555

Eduard Panther G (Dragon) No. 35557

Eduard Panther A *Schürzen* (Italeri) No. 35561

Eduard Panther A *Schürzen Zimmerit* (Italeri) No. 35562

Eduard Panther A *Zimmerit* (Italeri) No. 35563

Eduard Panther G *Schürzen* (Dragon) No. 35582

Eduard Panther Ausf. G *Schürzen* (Tamiya) No. 35597

Eduard Panther Ausf. D (ICM) No. 35841

Eduard Panther Ausf. D *Zimmerit* (ICM) No. 35851

Eduard Panther Ausf. A – Grilles (Dragon) No. TP002

Eduard Panther Ausf. A (Italeri) No. TP058

Eduard Panther Ausf. D (Dragon) No. TP059

Eduard Panther Ausf. G (Dragon) No. TP064

Gum Ka Panther Ausf. A/D basic photo-etched parts No. T-05

Gum Ka Panther Ausf. A equip photo-etched parts No. T-06

Gum Ka Dragon Panther Ausf. D exterior photo-etched Parts No. T-07

Lion Roar Panther G Early/Late photo-etched No. 35007

Lion Roar Panther A/D photo-etched (Dragon) No. 35022

Part Sd.Kfz.171 Panther Ausf. A (Dragon) No. P35065

Part Sd.Kfz.171 Panther Ausf. D/A – Fenders (Dragon) No. P35066

Part Panther Ausf. D/A Side Skirts (Dragon) No. P35067

Part Pz.Kpfw.V Panther – Track Horns (Dragon) No. P35068

Part Sd.Kfz.171 Panther Ausf. A/D – Grilles (Dragon) No. P35069

Part Sd.Kfz.172 Panther Ausf. D (Dragon) No. P35071

The Show Modelling Panther Ausf. G detail parts set (Tamiya) No. 061

The Show Modelling Panther Ausf. A detail parts set (Italeri) No. 062

The Show Modelling Panther Ausf. A photo-etched set (Dragon) No. 103

Voyager Model Panther V Ausf. A/D Side Skirts (Dragon) No. 35027

Voyager Model Panther V Ausf. G & Jagdpanther Side Skirts (Tamiya) No. 35028

Voyager Model Panther V & Jagdpanther Stowage Bin No. 35029

Voyager Model Panther V Ausf. A/D Antiaircraft Armor No. 35030

Resin *Zimmerit* sets

Atak *Zimmerit* for Sd.Kfz.171 Panther G No. 35006

Atak *Zimmerit* for SdKfz.171 Panther A (Late) No. 35019

Atak *Zimmerit* for SdKfz.171 Panther A (Late)
No. 35021
Atak *Zimmerit* for Bergepanther No. 35023
Atak *Zimmerit* for Sd.Kfz.171 Panther (1) No. 35027
Atak *Zimmerit* for Sd.Kfz.171 Panther (2) No. 35028
Cavalier Panther G Fruhe Version *Zimmerit*
(Horizontal Pattern) for Tamiya No. 0103
Cavalier Panther G Fruhe Version *Zimmerit* (Tile
Pattern) for Tamiya No. 0104
Cavalier Panther A *Zimmerit* (Horizontal Pattern) for
Italeri No. 0105
Cavalier Panther A *Zimmerit* (Tile Pattern) for Italeri
No. 0106
Cavalier Panther D *Zimmerit* (Diamond Pattern) for
Italeri No. 0123
Cavalier Panther A *Zimmerit* (Early Version) for
Dragon No. 0123

Aluminium barrels

Aber Panther A/D – Metal Gun Barrel No 35L04
Aber barrel for Panther G Late No. 35L36
Armo Turned-Metal Gun Barrel for Panther A
No. 35761
Armo Turned-Metal Gun Barrel for Panther A
No. 35762
Armo Turned-Metal Gun Barrel for Panther G
No. 35763
Armo Turned-Metal Gun Barrel for Panther D
No. 35764
Armorscale Gun Barrel for German tank Pz.Kpfw.V
Panther Ausf. G Late (Kin Type) No. B35-016
Armorscale Gun Barrel for German tank Pz.Kpfw.V
Panther Ausf. D and early A. No. B35-001
Eduard Panther G No. 34001
Eduard Panther A Early No. 34018
Eduard Barrel for Panther G No. 34057
Fine Molds Replacement Tank Gun Barrel for Panther
No. MG40
Fine Molds Replacement Tank Gun Barrel for Panther
A No. MG45D
Model Point Panther 7.5 cm KwK 42 Gun Barrel
No. 3530
Model Point MG-34 Machine-Gun Barrels (tank
variant) No. 35100

Track and wheel sets

Friulmodel Panther Late-Type tracks No. ATL-08
Friulmodel Panther Ausf. D No. ATL-33
Friulmodel Panther Drive Sprocket No. AW-13
Friulmodel Panther Idler No. AW-19
Modeling Artisan Mori Panther series Drive Sprockets
No. MGP05
Modelkasten Panther Tracks (Late Type) No. KK-1
Modelkasten Panther Ausf. D Tracks No. KK-28
Modelkasten Panther Ausf. D Roadwheel set
No. KW-3

Modelkasten Panther Late Track set (workable) SK-10
Modelkasten Panther Early Track set (workable) SK-13
Modelkasten Panther Late Spare Track set (workable)
SK-15

Interior sets

CMD Panther Radiator Cooling Fan and Radiators
insert No. CMD-040
CMK Pz.V Panther – Engine set (Tamiya) No. 3028
CMK Pz.V Panther – Driver's set (Tamiya) No. 3029
CMK Pz.V Panther – Interior set (Tamiya) No. 3030
Modeling Artisan Mori Panther Cupola No. MGP07
Modeling Artisan Mori Radiator Interior Panther A/D
No. MGP09
Royal Model Panther A Interior Details set 1 (Italeri)
No. 097
Royal Model Panther A Interior Details set 2 (Italeri)
No. 098
Verlinden Panther Ausf. A Interior No. 1965

Miscellaneous

Aber Early Model Shackle for Panther No. R14
Aber Late Model Shackle for Panther No. R16
Aber Cleaning Rod and Spare Aerial Stowage for
German Panther & Jagdpanther No. 35R23
Fine Molds German Fender Poles for Panther A
No. MG46D
Modeling Artisan Mori Ball Mounts for Panther Ausf.
G & Jagdpanther No. MGP06
Modeling Artisan Mori Over Fenders for Panther A/D
No. MGP08
Modeling Artisan Mori German AFV Tools
No. MGP14
Modeling Artisan Mori German 20-ton Jack set
No. MGP15
Modeling Artisan Mori Early Tow Mount for Panther
A. No. MGP16
Modeling Artisan Mori German Bosch Headlight set
No. MGP17
Modeling Artisan Mori Panther Strengthened Mantlet
No. MGP18
Moskit Panther A Exhausts No. 35-01
Moskit Panther D Exhaust No. 35-02
Moskit Panther G Exhaust No. 35-03
Moskit Bergepanther Ausf. A Exhaust No. 35-25
CMK Ammo set for Panther No. 3042
Profikit Ammo set for Panther No. 5502
Tamiya German Panther 75mm Ammo set No. 35173
Karaya Tow Cable for Pz.V Panther No. TCR01

Index

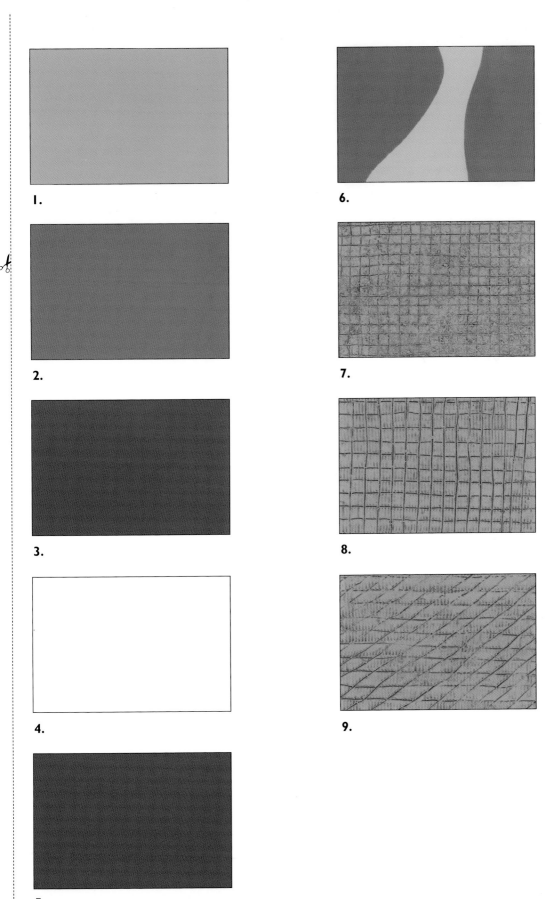

1.

2.

3.

4.

5.

6.

7.

8.

9.

6. Basecoat of *dunkelgrün* RAL 6003 with a hardedge camouflage scheme of *dunkelgelb* RAL 7028

At the same time that *dunkelgrün* RAL 6003 became the base colour, RAL 7028 and RAL 8017 were applied with sharp contours to create a camouflage pattern. It appears that sometimes only one of these colours was applied over the base coat. Vallejo Model Air Dark Yellow (025) and Sand (075) were mixed together at a 3:1 ratio and sprayed on top of Vallejo Model Air Panzer Olive Green 1943 (096) on the Panther Ausf. G model.

7. *Zimmerit* pattern consisting of a roughly applied paste with horizontal and vertical lines scored though it

This pattern of *Zimmerit* was a pattern typically seen on vehicles produced by Daimler-Benz. To replicate this pattern Mori Mori two-part polyester putty was used along with a sponge and homemade scoring tool.

8. *Zimmerit* pattern consisting of a vertically ridged paste with horizontal and vertical lines scored though it

This pattern of vertical ridges overlayed with horizontally and vertically scored lines was typical of the type found on MAN-produced vehicles.

9. *Zimmerit* pattern consisting of a vertically ridged paste with horizontal and diagonal lines scored though it

A variation of the typical MAN pattern with diagonally instead of vertically scored lines. This pattern is often seen on the rear stowage bins, front fenders or turrets.

1. *Dunkelgelb* RAL 7028

Starting in February 1943 the base paint was changed to *dunkelgelb* RAL 7028. Tamiya Dark Yellow (XF-60) lightened with a little Flat White (XF-2) at a ratio of 3:1, was used to create this colour.

2. *Dunkelgrün* RAL 6003

Initially this colour was applied to German AFVs as part of the three-colour camouflage scheme. In late 1944 this was to become the base colour itself. Vallejo Model Air Panzer Olive Green 1943 (096), which comes pre-thinned, was used for this colour.

3. *Rotbraun* RAL 8017

In conjunction with RAL 6003 this colour was to be field-applied over the base colour. Tamiya Red Brown (XF-64) was used thinned with isopropyl alcohol and sprayed through an airbrush at low pressure (10-15psi).

4. *Elfenbein* RAL 1001

This colour was used on the interior of most German close-topped AFVs. A suitable colour match was made from Vallejo Model Air White (001) mixed with about 30 per cent Sand (075).

5. Red Primer RAL 8012

This colour was applied as the initial preservative layer of paint on German AFVs. Floquil Oxide Red was used, thinned with mineral spirits, to replicate this colour.